TWIN TOWERS

The original World Trade Center was a large complex of seven building in Lower Manhattan. The Twin Towers were two of those even building.

1,730 feet (530 m)
110 Stories

4

People running to escape the smoke and debris from the World Trade Center Collapsing.

Debris at St. Paul's church.

A tire from one of the hijacked planes lies in the street near the destroyed World Trade Center. (Church and Wall St.)

Looking West from Fulton and Broadway.

St. Paul's Chapel

10

Double Check

Seward Johnson's 1982 sculpture, "Double Check" for Zuccotti Park (formerly called Liberty Plaza Park) shows a very lifelike "everyman" businessman sitting in the park. The bronze businessman sculpture survived the September 11, 2001 terrorist attacks of the nearby World Trade Center covered in debris bearing scratches and bruises. Johnson has called his sculpture an iconic "stand-in" for those who didn't make it, a poignant reminder of hope and endurance for us all. Zuccotti Park is located in Lower Manhattan near the World Trade Center, and is bounded by Broadway, Trinity, Liberty and Cedar Streets.

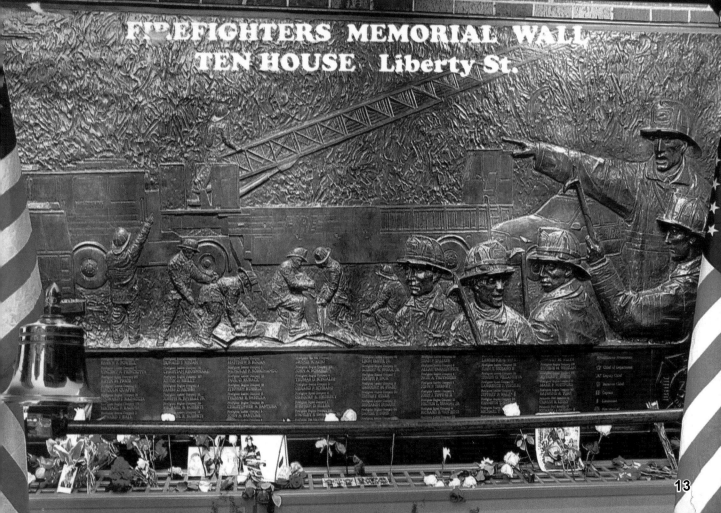

FIREFIGHTERS MEMORIAL WALL
TEN HOUSE Liberty St.

13

34

F.D.N.Y.

343 FIREFIGHTERS PERISHED ON 9/11
(Including a chaplain and two paramedics) of the New York
City Fire Department (FDNY).

IN LOVING MEMORY

✈ Paul Friedman ✈ Karleton D.B. Fyfe ✈ Peter Gay ✈ Linda George ✈ Edmund Glazer ✈ Lisa Fenn Gordenstein ✈ Andrew Peter Char
nn Neira ✈ Renee Newell ✈ Jacqueline J. Norton ✈ Robert Grant Norton ✈ Jane M. Orth ✈ Thomas Pecorelli ✈ Berinthia Berenson
Marchand ✈ Capt. Victor Saracini ✈ Michael C. Tarrou ✈ Alicia Nicole Titus ✈ Alona Avraham ✈ Garnet Edward 'Ace' Bailey ✈ Mar
F. Hardacre ✈ Eric Samadikan Hartono ✈ James E. Hayden ✈ Herbert Wilson Homer ✈ Robert Adrien Jalbert ✈ Ralph Francis Kers
de Center ‖ Gordon McCannel Aamoth ‖ Maria Rose Abad ‖ Edelmiro 'Ed' Abad ‖ Andrew Anthony Abate ‖ Vincent Abate ‖ Laurence
hladiotis ‖ Shabbir Ahmed ‖ Terrance Andre Aiken ‖ Godwin Ajala ‖ Gertrude M. Alagero ‖ Andrew Alameno ‖ Margaret 'Peggy' Je
pher Charles Amoroso ‖ Kazuhiro Anai ✠FF. Calixto Charlie Anaya ‖ Jorge Octavio Santos Anaya ‖ Joseph Peter Anchundia ‖ Kermit C
ee ✠FF. Carl Asaro ‖ Michael A. Asciak ‖ Michael Edward Asher ‖ Janice Ashley ‖ Thomas J. Ashton ‖ Manuel O. Asitimbay ✠Lt. Gregg Af
arbella ‖ Ivan Kyrillos Fairbanks Barbosa ‖ Victor Daniel Barbosa ‖ Colleen Ann Barkow ‖ David Michael Barkway ✠FF. Matthew E. Ba
man ‖ Maria Behr ‖ Yelena Belilovsky ‖ Nina Patrice Bell ‖ Andrea Della Bella ‖ Debbie S. Bellows ✠FF. Stephen Elliot Belson ‖ Paul M
rvaney ‖ Bella Bhukhan ‖ Shimmy D. Biegeleisen ✠FF. Peter Alexander Bielfeld ‖ William Biggart ✠FF. Brian Bilcher ✠FF. Carl Vincent B
eur ‖ Colin Arthur Bonnett ✠FF. Frank Bonomo ‖ Yvonne L. Bonomo ‖ Sean Booker ‖ Sherry Ann Bordeaux ‖ Krystine C. Bordenabe ‖ M
chael Breitweiser ‖ Edward A. Brennan ‖ Frank H. Brennan ✠FF. Michael Emmett Brennan ✠FF. Peter Brennan ‖ Thomas M. Brennan ✠
ga ‖ Stephen Bunin ‖ Thomas Daniel Burke ✠Capt. William F. Burke, Jr. ‖ Matthew J. Burke ✠Asst. Chief Donald James Burns ‖ Kathle
by' Calixte ✠Capt. Frank J. Callahan ✠PO. Liam Callahan ‖ Luigi Calvi ‖ Roko Camaj ✠FF. Michael F. Cammarata ‖ David Otey Campbell ‖ G
en Carney ‖ Joyce Ann Carpeneto ‖ Alicia Acevedo Carranza ‖ Jeremy M. Carrington ✠FF. Michael T. Carroll ✠FF. Peter J. Carroll ‖ Ja
celic ‖ Ana M. Centeno ‖ Joni Cesta ‖ Jeffrey M. Chairnoff ‖ Swarna Chalasani ‖ William Chalcoff ‖ Eli Chalouh ‖ Charles Lawrence
Salahuddin Chowdhury ‖ Kirsten L. Christophe ‖ Pamela Chu ‖ Steven Paul Chucknick ‖ Wai-ching Chung ‖ Christopher Ciafardini ‖ Alex
hew Coffey ‖ Florence Cohen ‖ Kevin Sanford Cohen ‖ Lawrence Cohen ‖ Anthony Joseph Coladonato ‖ Mark J. Colaio ‖ Stephen J. Co
nnolly ‖ Cynthia L. Connolly ‖ James Lee Connor ‖ Jonathan 'J.C.' Connors ‖ Kevin P. Connors ‖ Kevin Francis Conroy ‖ Brenda E. Conw
e ‖ Andre Cox ‖ Frederick John Cox ✠FF. James Raymond Coyle ‖ Michelle Coyle-Eulau ‖ Anne M. Martino Cramer ‖ Christopher Seton
mas Cummins ‖ Nilton Albuquerque Fernao Cunha ‖ Michael Joseph Cunningham ✠FF. Robert Curatolo ‖ Laurence Curia ‖ Paul Dar
tthew Davidson ‖ Titus Davidson ‖ Niurka Davila ✠PO. Clinton Davis ‖ Wayne Terrial Davis ‖ Calvin Dawson ‖ Anthony Richard Dawson
N. DeMeo ‖ Francis X. Deming ‖ Carol K. Demitz ‖ Kevin Dennis ‖ Thomas F. Dennis ‖ Jean C. DePalma ‖ Jose Nicolas Depena ‖ Robert J. D
ot Dickey ‖ Lawrence Patrick Dickinson ‖ Michael David Diehl ‖ John DiFato ‖ Vincent F. DiFazio ‖ Carl DiFranco ‖ Donald J. DiFran
hristopher Dowdell ‖ Mary Yolanda Dowling ✠Dep. Chief Raymond M. Downey ‖ Joseph M. Doyle ‖ Frank Joseph Doyle ‖ Randy Drake
dy Edwards ‖ Lisa Egan ✠Capt. Martin J. Egan ‖ Michael Egan ‖ Christine Egan ‖ Samantha Egan ‖ Carole Eggert ‖ Lisa Caren Weinste
Evans ✠FF. Robert Edward Evans ‖ Meredith Emily June Ewart ‖ Catherine K. Fagan ‖ Patricia M. Fagan ✠EMT Keith G. Fairben ‖ Willia
n ‖ Francis J. 'Frank' Feely ‖ Garth E. Feeney ‖ Sean B. Fegan ✠FF. Lee S. Fehling ‖ Peter Feidelberg ✠FF. Alan David Feinberg ‖ Rosa
✠Capt. John R. Fischer ‖ Andrew Fisher ‖ Thomas J. Fisher ‖ Bennett Lawson Fisher ‖ John Roger Fisher ‖ Lucy Fishman ‖ Ryan D. F
r ‖ Ana Fosteris ✠FF. Robert J. Foti ‖ Jeffrey L. Fox ‖ Virginia Fox ‖ Virgin 'Lucy' Francis ‖ Pauline Francis ‖ Joan Francis ‖ Gary J. Fra
Galante ‖ Grace Galante ‖ Anthony Edward Gallagher ‖ Daniel James Gallagher ‖ John Patrick Gallagher ‖ Cono E. Gallo ‖ Vincent G
Gary ‖ Palmina Delli Gatti ‖ Boyd A. Gatton ‖ Donald Richard Gavagan ‖ Terence D. Gazzani ✠FF. Gary Paul Geidel ‖ Paul Hamilton Ge
ul Gilbert ‖ Paul Stuart Gilbey ✠FF. Paul John Gill ‖ Mark Y. Gilles ‖ Evan H. Gillette ‖ Ronald Gilligan ✠Sgt. Rodney C. Gillis ‖ Laura
tein ‖ Steven Goldstein ‖ Andrew H. Golkin ‖ Dennis James Gomes ‖ Enrique Antonio Gomez ‖ Jose Bienvenido Gomez ‖ Manuel Gomez ‖ Wi
r Grayling ‖ John Michael Grazioso ‖ Timothy Grazioso ‖ Derrick Arthur Green ‖ Wade Brian Green ‖ Elaine Myra Greenberg ‖ Gayle R
P. Gullickson ‖ Babita Guman ‖ Douglas B. Gurian ‖ Philip T. Guza ‖ Barbara Guzzardo ‖ Peter Gyulavary ‖ Gary Robert Haag ‖ Andr
P. Hannafin ‖ Kevin James Hannaford ‖ Michael L. Hannan ✠FF. Dana Rey Hannon ‖ Vassilios G. Haramis ‖ James A. Haran ‖ Jeffrey P.
Haynes ‖ Scott Jordan Hazelcorn ✠Lt. Michael K. Healey ‖ Roberta Bernstein Heber ‖ Charles Francis Xavier Heeran ✠FF. John F. He
B. Higgins ‖ Robert D. Higley ‖ Todd Russell Hill ‖ Clara Victorine Hinds ‖ Neal Hinds ‖ Mark D. Hindy ‖ Richard Bruce Van Hine ‖ Katsuyu
n ‖ Matthew D. Horning ‖ Robert L. Horohoe ‖ Aaron Horwitz ‖ Charles J. Houston ✠PO. Uhuru G. Houston ✠PO. George G. Howard ‖ Mic
derick J. Ill Jr. ‖ Abraham Nethanel Ilowitz ✠Insp. Anthony P. Infante, Jr. ‖ Louis S. Inghilterra ‖ Christopher N. Ingrassia ‖ Paul Inn
an-Pierre ‖ Maxima Jean-Pierre ‖ Paul E. Jeffers ‖ Joseph Jenkins ‖ Alan K. Jensen ‖ Prem N. Jerath ‖ Farah Jeudy ‖ Hweidar Jian ‖ El
san Juday ‖ The Rev. Mychal Judge OFM ✠PO. Paul W. Jurgens ‖ Sco. Thomas Edward Jurgens ‖ Kacinga Kabeya ‖ Shashi Kiran Lakshmi
Keasler ✠FF. Paul Hanlon Keating ‖ Leo Russell Keene ‖ Joseph J. Keller ‖ Peter Rodney Kellerman ‖ Joseph P. Kellett ‖ Frederick
oon Kim ‖ Lawrence Don Kim ‖ Mary Jo Kimelman ‖ Andrew Marshall King ‖ Lucille T. King ✠FF. Robert C. King Jr. ‖ Lisa M. King-Johnso
tic ‖ Danielle Kousoulis ‖ John J. Kren ✠FF. William E. Krukowski ‖ Lyudmila Ksido ‖ Shekhar Kumar ‖ Fire Marshall Kenneth B. Kumpe
T. Lane ‖ Brendan M. Lang ‖ Rosanne P. Lang ‖ Vanessa Langer ‖ Mary Lou Langley ✠FF. Peter J. Langone ✠PO. Thomas Langone ‖ Mich
PO. James Patrick Leahy ✠Lt. Joseph Gerard Leavey ✠FF. Neil J. Leavy ‖ Leon Lebor ‖ Kenneth Charles Ledee ‖ Alan J. Lederman ‖
Antoine Lesperance ‖ Jeffrey Earle LeVeen ✠PO. John D. Levi ‖ Neil D. Levin ‖ Alisha Caren Levin ‖ Robert Levine ‖ Robert M. Levine
zcano ‖ Martin Lizzul ‖ George A. Llanes ‖ Elizabeth Claire Logler ‖ Catherine Lisa Loguidice ‖ Jerome Robert Lohez ‖ Michael W. Lo
gin ‖ Farrell Peter Lynch ✠PO. James Francis Lynch ‖ Louise A. Lynch ‖ Michael Lynch ✠Lt. Michael F. Lynch ✠FF. Michael Francis
moto ‖ Abdu Malahi ‖ Debora Maldonado ‖ Myrna T. Maldonado-Agosto ‖ Alfred R. Maler ‖ Gregory James Malone ‖ Edward Francis
rtello ‖ Michael A. Marti ✠Lt. Peter C. Martin ‖ William J. Martin ‖ Brian E. Martineau ‖ Betsy Martinez ‖ Edward J. Martinez ‖ Jose
ro ‖ Nancy T. Mauro ‖ Tyrone May ✠FF. Keithroy M. Maynard ‖ Robert J. Mayo ✠Capt. Kathy Mazza-Delosh ‖ Edward Mazzella ‖ Jenni
McDonnell ‖ Michael McDonnell ‖ John F. McDowell ‖ Eamon J. McEneaney ‖ John Thomas McErlean ‖ Daniel F. McGinley ‖ Mark Rya
ert C. McLaughlin ‖ George Patrick McLaughlin ‖ Gavin McMahon ✠FF. Robert Dismas McMahon ‖ Edmund M. McNally ‖ Daniel McNeal
vannah Mena ✠FF. Charles R. Mendez ‖ Lizette Mendoza ‖ Shevonne Mentis ✠FF. Steve J. Mercado ‖ Wesley Mercer ‖ Ralph Joseph Merc
r ‖ Benjamin Millman ‖ Charles M. Mills ‖ Ronald Keith Milstein ✠FF. Robert J. Minara ‖ William G. Minardi ‖ Louis Joseph Minervino ‖
tano ✠FF. Michael G. Montesi ‖ Cheryl Ann Monyak ✠Capt. Thomas C. Moody ‖ Sharon Moore ‖ Krishna Moorthy ‖ Abner Morales ‖ Ca
vid Moskal ‖ Manuel Da Mota ‖ Marco Motroni ‖ Iouri A. Mouchinski ‖ Jude J. Moussa ‖ Peter C. Moutos ‖ Damion Mowatt ✠FF. Christo
urphy ‖ Patrick Sean Murphy ✠Lt. Raymond E. Murphy ‖ Charles Murphy ‖ John Joseph Murray ‖ John Joseph Murray ‖ Susan D. Mu
llen Nelson ‖ Oscar Nesbitt ✠FF. Gerard Terence Nevins ‖ Christopher Newton-Carter ‖ Kapinga Ngalula ‖ Nancy Yuen Ngo ‖ Jody T
rien ✠Captain Daniel O'Callaghan ‖ Richard J. O'Connor ‖ Dennis J. O'Connor ‖ Diana J. O'Connor ‖ Keith K. O'Connor ‖ Amy O'Doher
imothy O'Mahony ‖ Toshihiro Onda ‖ Seamus L. Oneal ‖ John P. O'Neill ‖ Sean Gordon Corbett O'Neill ‖ Peter J. O'Neill ‖ Michael C. O
a ‖ Angel M. Pabon ‖ Israel Pabon ‖ Roland Pacheco ‖ Michael Benjamin Packer ‖ Deepa K. Pakkala ✠FF. Jeffrey A. Palazzo ‖ Thomas A
arkes ‖ Robert Emmett Parks ‖ Hasmukhrai Chuckulal Parmar ✠FF. Robert A. Parro ‖ Diane Marie Moore Parsons ‖ Leobardo Lopez Pas
lino ‖ Michel Adrian Pelletier ‖ Anthony Peluso ‖ Angel Ramon Pena ‖ Richard Al Penny ‖ Salvatore F. Pepe ‖ Carl Allen Peralta ‖ Ro
th John Phelan ‖ Michael V. San Phillip ‖ Eugenia Pantieri ‖ Ludwig John Picarro ‖ Matthew Picerno ‖ Joseph O. Pick ✠FF. Christoph
oulos ‖ Brandon Jerome Powell ✠FF. Shawn Edward Powell ‖ Tony Pratt ‖ Gregory M. Preziose ‖ Wanda Ivelisse Prince ✠FF. Vincent
iggio ‖ Laura Marie Ragonese-Snik ✠FF. Michael P. Ragusa ‖ Peter F. Raimondi ‖ Harry A. Raines ‖ Ehtesham U. Raja ‖ Valsa Raju ✠FF. E
ese ✠FF. Donald J. Regan ✠Lt. Robert M. Regan ‖ Thomas M. Regan ✠FF. Christian Michael Otto Regenhard ‖ Howard Reich ‖ Gregg
D. Richards ‖ Gregory Richards ‖ Venesha O. Richards ✠FF. James C. Riches ‖ Alan Jay Richman ‖ John M. Rigo ‖ Theresa 'Ginger' Risc
dak ✠PO. Antonio Jose Carrusca Rodrigues ✠FF. Anthony Rodriguez ‖ Carmen Milagros Rodriguez ‖ Marsha A. Rodriguez ✠PO. Richa
osenblum ‖ Joshua A. Rosenthal ‖ Richard David Rosenthal ‖ Daniel Rosetti ‖ Norman Rossinow ✠FF. Nicholas P. Rossomando ‖ Micha
aada ‖ Jason E. Sabbag ✠FF. Thomas E. Sabella ‖ Scott Saber ‖ Joseph Sacerdote ‖ Mohammad Ali Sadeque ‖ Francis J. Sadocha ‖ Jud
ler ‖ James Sands ‖ Ayleen J. Santiago ‖ Kirsten Santiago ‖ Maria Theresa Santillan ‖ Susan G. Santo ✠FF. Christopher A. Santora ✠F
hlissel ‖ Karen Helene Schmidt ‖ Ian Schneider ✠FF. Thomas G. Schoales ‖ Marisa Di Nardo Schorpp ‖ Frank G. Schott ✠FF. Gerard P. Sc
ova ‖ Adele Sessa ‖ Sita Nermalla Sewnarine ‖ Karen Lynn Seymour-Dietrich ‖ Davis 'Deeg' Sezna ‖ Thomas Joseph Sgroi ‖ Jayesh Sha
verstein ‖ Nasima H. Simjee ‖ Bruce Edward Simmons ‖ Arthur Simon ‖ Paul Joseph Simon ‖ Kenneth Alan Simon ‖ Michael John Simon ‖
Karl Trumbull Smith ✠FF. Kevin J. Smith ✠FF. Leon Smith, Jr. ✠PO. Moira Smith ‖ Rosemary A. Smith ‖ Sandra Fajardo Smith ‖ Jeffrey
P. Spor Jr. ‖ Klaus Johannes Sprockamp ‖ Saranya Srinuan ‖ Michael F. Stabile ✠Bat. Chief Lawrence T. Stack ✠Capt. Timothy M. St
ne ‖ Jimmy Nevill Storey ‖ Timothy Stout ‖ Thomas S. Strada ‖ James J. Straine ‖ Edward W. Straub ‖ George Strauch ‖ Edward T. Str
Swensen ‖ Thomas F. Swift ‖ Derek O. Sword ‖ Kevin T. Szocik ‖ Gina Sztejnberg ‖ Norbert P. Szurkowski ‖ Harry Taback ‖ Joann Tabeel
egtmeier ‖ Yeshavant Moreshwar Tembe ‖ Anthony Tempesta ‖ Dorothy Temple ‖ Stanley L. Temple ‖ David Tengelin ‖ Brian J. Terrenzi ‖
nk Tipaldi ✠FF. John J. Tipping II ‖ David Tirado ✠FF. Hector Luis Tirado, Jr. ‖ Michelle Titolo ‖ John J. Tobin ‖ Richard J. Todisco ‖ Vla
ph Tuzio ‖ Robert T. Twomey ‖ Jennifer Tzemis ‖ John G. Ueltzhoeffer ‖ Tyler V. Ugolyn ‖ Michael A. Uliano ‖ Jonathan J. Uman ‖ Anil Shi
Velamuri ‖ Jorge Velazquez ✠FF. Lawrence G. Veling ‖ Anthony M. Ventura ‖ David Vera ‖ Loretta Ann Vero ‖ Christopher J. Vialonga ‖
ctor Wald ‖ Benjamin Walker ‖ Glen J. Wall ✠Sco. Mitchel Scott Wallace ✠Lt. Robert F. Wallace ‖ Roy Michael Wallace ‖ Peter G. Wa
el T. Weinberg ‖ Steven Weinberg ‖ Scott Jeffrey Weingard ‖ Steven Weinstein ‖ Simon Weiser ‖ David T. Weiss ✠FF. David M. Weiss ‖
‖ Alison Marie Wildman ✠Lt. Glenn E. Wilkinson ‖ John C. Willett ‖ Brian Patrick Williams ‖ Crossley Williams ‖ David Williams ‖ De
g Wong ‖ Yin Ping 'Steven' Wong ‖ Brent James Woodall ‖ James J. Woods ‖ Patrick Woods ‖ Richard Herron Woodwell ✠Capt. David Te
n Zampieri ‖ Mark Zangrilli ‖ Ira Zaslow ‖ Kenneth Albert Zelman ‖ Abraham J. Zelmanowitz ‖ Martin Morales Zempoaltecatl ‖ Zhe 'Ze
er ✈ Asia Cottom ✈ James Debeuneure ✈ Rodney Dickens ✈ Eddie Dillard ✈ Charles Droz ✈ Barbara G. Edwards ✈ Charles S. Falke
opper ✈ Robert Speisman ✈ Norma Lang Steuerle ✈ Hilda E. Taylor ✈ Leonard Taylor ✈ Sandra Teague ✈ Leslie A. Whittington ✈ Jo
vis ✪ Capt. Gerald Francis Deconto ✪ Lt. Col. Jerry Don Dickerson ✪ Johnnie Doctor ✪ Capt. Robert Edward Dolan ✪ Cmdr. William Ho
Hymel ✪ Sgt. Maj. Lacey B. Ivory ✪ Lt. Col. Dennis M. Johnson ✪ Judith Jones ✪ Brenda Kegler ✪ Lt. Michael Scott Lamana ✪ David W. Lay
artin Panik ✪ Maj. Clifford L. Patterson ✪ Lt. J.G. Darin Howard Pontell ✪ Scott Powell ✪ 'Retired' Capt. Jack Punches ✪ Joseph John
tatz ✪ Edna L. Stephens ✪ Sgt. Maj. Larry Strickland ✪ Maj. Kip P. Taylor ✪ Sandra C. Taylor ✪ Karl W. Teepe ✪ Sgt. Tamara Thur

OF THE BRAVE AND

AI ✠ BETTY ONG ✠ JEAN ROGER ✠ DIANNE SNYDER ✠ MADELINE SWEENEY ✠ ANNA S. W. ALLISON ✠ DAVID ANGELL ✠ LYNN ANGELL ✠ SEIMA AOYAM
ETER HASHEM ✠ ROBERT HAYES ✠ EDWARD 'TED' R. HENNESSY JR. ✠ JOHN A. HOFER ✠ CORA HIDALGO HOLLAND ✠ NICHOLAS HUMBER ✠ WALEED
ALES PUOPOLO ✠ DAVID E. RETIK ✠ PHILIP M. ROSENZWEIG ✠ RICHARD ROSS ✠ JESSICA SACHS ✠ RAHMA SALIE ✠ HEATHER LEE SMITH ✠ DOUGL
DREW BERKELEY ✠ TOURI BOLOURCHI ✠ KLAUS BOTHE ✠ DANIEL R. BRANDHORST ✠ DAVID REED GAMBOA BRANDHORST ✠ JOHN BRETT CAHILL ✠
IG ✠ BRIAN KEVIN KINNEY ✠ ROBERT GEORGE LEBLANC ✠ MACLOVIO LOPEZ ✠ MARIANNE MACFARLANE ✠ LOUIS NEIL MARIANI ✠ JULIANA VALE
WILLIAM F. ABRAHAMSON ‖ RICHARD ANTHONY ACETO ‖ ERICA VAN ACKER ‖ HEINRICH B. ACKERMANN ‖ PAUL ANDREW ACQUAVIVA ‖ DONALD L. A
ALBERO ‖ JON L. ALBERT ‖ PETER CRAIG ALDERMAN ‖ JACQUELYN DELAINE ALDRIDGE ‖ GRACE ALEGRE-CUA ‖ DAVID D. ALGER ‖ ERNEST ALIKAK
YVETTE ANDERSON ‖ JOHN ANDREACCHIO ‖ MICHAEL ROURKE ANDREWS ‖ JEAN A. ANDRUCKI ‖ SIEW-NYA ANG ✠FF. JOSEPH ANGELINI JR. ✠FF. JOSE
ALD ATWOOD ‖ JAMES AUDIFFRED ‖ KENNETH W. VAN AUKEN ‖ LOUIS F. AVERSANO JR. ‖ EZRA AVILES ‖ AYODE ‖ AWE ‖ SAMUEL 'SANDY' AYALA ‖ ARLI
BARNES ‖ EVAN J. BARON ‖ RENEE BARRETT-ARJUNE ✠FF. ARTHUR T. BARRY ‖ DIANE G. BARRY ✠PO. MAURICE VINCENT BARRY ‖ SCOTT D. BART ‖
ENISE LENORE BENEDETTO ‖ BRYAN CRAIG BENNETT ‖ OLIVER DUNCAN BENNETT ‖ ERIC L. BENNETT ‖ MARGARET L. BENSON ‖ DOMINICK J. BERAR
A DAVID BIRNBAUM ‖ GEORGE BISHOP ‖ JEFFREY D. BITTNER ‖ BALEWA ALBERT BLACKMAN ✠FF. CHRISTOPHER JOSEPH BLACKWELL ‖ SUSAN L. BLAI
VSKI ‖ RICHARD E. BOSCO ‖ JOHN HOWARD BOULTON ‖ FRANCISCO BOURDIER ‖ THOMAS H. BOWDEN ‖ KIMBERLY S. BOWERS ‖ VERONIQUE 'BONNIE' N
EL ‖ GARY L. BRIGHT ‖ JONATHAN ERIC BRILEY ‖ MARK A. BRISMAN ‖ PAUL GARY BRISTOW ‖ VICTORIA ALVAREZ BRITO ‖ MARK FRANCIS BRODERICK ‖
AMES BURNS ✠FF. JOHN PATRICK BURNSIDE ‖ IRINA BUSLO ‖ MILTON BUSTILLO ✠FF. THOMAS M. BUTLER ✠FF. PATRICK D. BYRNE ‖ TIMOTHY G. BY
PBELL ‖ SANDRA PATRICIA CAMPBELL ‖ JILL MARIE CAMPBELL ‖ ROBERT ARTHUR CAMPBELL ‖ JUAN ORTEGA CAMPOS ‖ SEAN CANAVAN ‖ JOHN A. CAN
S MARCEL CARTIER ‖ VIVIAN CASALDUC ‖ JOHN F. CASAZZA ‖ PAUL CASCIO ‖ KATHLEEN HUNT CASEY ‖ MARGARITO CASILLAS ✠FF. THOMAS ANTHONY
CHANG ‖ MARK L. CHARETTE ‖ GREGORIO MANUEL CHAVEZ ‖ JAYCERYLL M. DE CHAVEZ ‖ PETE 'FRANK' CHECO ‖ DOUGLAS MACMILLAN CHERRY ‖ S
ANN CILENTE ‖ ELAINE CILLO ‖ EDNA CINTRON ‖ NESTOR ANDRE CINTRON ✠LT. ROBERT DOMINICK CIRRI EMS ‖ JUAN PABLO ALVAREZ CISNEROS ‖ GR
M. COLASANTI ‖ MICHEL PARIS COLBERT ‖ KEVIN NATHANIEL COLBERT ‖ KEITH EUGENE COLEMAN ‖ SCOTT THOMAS COLEMAN ✠FF. TAREL COLEMAN
OOK ‖ HELEN D. COOK ‖ JOHN A. COOPER ‖ JOSEPH J. COPPO ‖ GERARD J. COPPOLA ‖ JOSEPH ALBERT CORBETT ‖ ALEJANDRO CORDERO ✠FF. ROBE
NT ✠FF. ROBERT JAMES CRAWFORD ‖ JAMES L. CRAWFORD ‖ JOANNE MARY CREGAN ‖ LUCIA CRIFASI ✠LT. JOHN A. CRISCI ‖ DANIEL HAL CRISMAN
CURRY ✠SGT. MICHAEL SEAN CURTIN ‖ GAVIN CUSHNY ‖ CALEB ARRON DACK ‖ CARLOS S. DACOSTA ✠PO. JOHN D'ALLARA ‖ VINCENT D'AMADEO
DAY ‖ EMERITA 'EMY' DE LA PENA ‖ MELANIE LOUISE DE VERE ‖ WILLIAM T. DEAN ‖ ROBERT J. DEANGELIS ✠BAT. CHIEF THOMAS P. DEANGELIS ‖ TAR
RIENZO ✠FF. DAVID PAUL DERUBBIO ‖ JEMAL LEGESSE DESANTIS ‖ CHRISTIAN L. DESIMONE ‖ EDWARD DESIMONE ✠LT. ANDREW J. DESPERITO ‖ MI
ARTINO ‖ STEPHEN P. DIMINO ‖ WILLIAM J. DIMMLING ‖ CHRISTOPHER DINCUFF ‖ JEFFREY M. DINGLE ‖ ANTHONY DIONISIO ✠FF. GEORGE DIPASQ
DRISCOLL ‖ MIRNA A. DUARTE ‖ LUKE A. DUDEK ‖ CHRISTOPHER MICHAEL DUFFY ✠FF. GERARD J. DUFFY ‖ MICHAEL JOSEPH DUFFY ‖ THOMAS W.
NST 'JACK' EICHLER ‖ ERIC ADAM EISENBERG ‖ DAPHNE F. ELDER ✠FF. MICHAEL J. ELFERIS ✠PO. MARK J. ELLIS ‖ VALERIE SILVER ELLIS ‖ ALBERT
FALLON ‖ ANTHONY J. FALLONE ‖ DOLORES B. FANELLI ✠BAT. CHIEF JOHN JOSEPH FANNING ‖ KATHLEEN 'KIT' FARAGHER ✠BAT. CHIEF THOMAS F.
WARD T. FERGUS ‖ GEORGE FERGUSON ‖ HENRY FERNANDEZ ‖ JUDY H. FERNANDEZ ‖ JOSE MANUEL CONTRERAS FERNANDEZ ‖ ELISA GISELLE FER
ITZPATRICK ‖ RICHARD P. FITZSIMONS ‖ SALVATORE A. FIUMEFREDDO ‖ CHRISTINA DONOVAN FLANNERY ‖ EILEEN FLECHA ‖ FIRE MARSHALL ANDR
PETER CHRISTOPHER FRANK ‖ RICHARD K. FRASER ‖ KEVIN JOSEPH FRAWLEY ‖ CLYDE FRAZIER ‖ LILLIAN I. FREDERICK ✠LT. ANDREW A. FREDERIC
WARD GALVIN ‖ GIOVANNA 'GENNI' GAMBALE ✠FF. THOMAS GAMBINO, JR. ‖ GIANN F. GAMBOA ‖ PETER J. GANCI, JR. ✠ CLAUDE MICHAEL GANN ✠LT. C
TER GELINAS ‖ STEVEN PAUL GELLER ‖ HOWARD G. GELLING ‖ PETER VICTOR GENCO JR. ‖ STEVEN GREGORY GENOVESE ‖ ALAYNE F. GENTUL ✠DEP. C
EY ✠FF. JEFFREY J. GIORDANO ✠FF. JOHN J. GIORDANO ‖ DONNA MARIE GIORDANO ‖ STEVEN A. GIORGETTI ‖ MARTIN GIOVINAZZO ‖ KUM-KUM GIROLA
ONZALEZ ‖ JOEL GUEVARA GONZALEZ ‖ ROSA J. GONZALEZ ‖ MAURICIO GONZALEZ ‖ CALVIN J. GOODING ‖ HARRY GOODY ‖ KIRAN REDDY GOPU ‖ CATH
THUR GREENLEAF ‖ EILEEN MARSHA GREENSTEIN ‖ ELIZABETH 'LISA' MARTIN GREGG ‖ DONALD H. GREGORY ‖ FLORENCE M. GREGORY ‖ DENISE GRE
ARBARA M. HABIB ‖ PHILIP HAENTZLER ‖ NIZAM A. HAFIZ ‖ KAREN ELIZABETH HAGERTY ‖ STEVEN HAGIS ‖ MARY LOU HAGUE ‖ LT. DAVID HALDER
N HARGRAVE ✠FF. DANIEL E. HARLIN ‖ FRANCES HAROS ✠LT. HARVEY L. HARRELL ✠LT. STEPHEN GARY HARRELL ‖ STEWART D. HARRIS ‖ AISHA A
EPH HELLER ‖ JOANN L. HELTIBRIDLE ‖ MARK F. HEMSCHOOT ✠FF. RONNIE LEE HENDERSON ‖ JANET HENDRICKS ‖ BRIAN HENNESSEY ‖ MICHELLE M
LIA HO ‖ TARA YVETTE HOBBS ‖ THOMAS A. HOBBS ‖ JAMES J. HOBIN ‖ ROBERT WAYNE HOBSON ‖ DAJUAN HODGES ‖ RONALD GEORGE HOERNER ‖ PA
EN L. HOWELL ‖ JENNIFER L. DORSEY-HOWLEY ‖ MILAGROS "MILLIE" HROMADA ‖ MARIAN HRYCAK ✠PO. STEPHEN HUCZKO ‖ KRIS R. HUGHES ‖ MELISS
RBY ‖ DOUGLAS IRGANG ‖ TODD A. ISAAC ‖ ERIK HANS ISBRANDTSEN ‖ TAIZO ISHIKAWA ‖ ARAM ISKENDERIAN ‖ JOHN ISKYAN ‖ KAZUSHIGE ITO ‖ AL
IMENEZ ‖ NICHOLAS JOHN ‖ CHARLES GREGORY JOHN ‖ SCOTT M. JOHNSON ‖ LASHAWANA JOHNSON ✠FF. WILLIAM R. JOHNSTON ‖ ARTHUR JOSE
KHAROY MUKHOMETOVNA KAMARDINOVA ‖ SHARI KANDELL ‖ HOWARD LEE KANE ‖ JENNIFER LYNN KANE ‖ FIRE MARSHALL VINCENT D. KANE ‖ JO
EPH KELLY ‖ JOSEPH A. KELLY ‖ MAURICE PATRICK KELLY ✠FF. RICHARD JOHN KELLY, JR. ‖ THOMAS MICHAEL KELLY ✠LT. THOMAS RICHARD KELLY
‖ CHRIS MICHAEL KIRBY ‖ HOWARD 'BARRY' KIRSCHBAUM ‖ GLENN DAVIS KIRWIN ‖ RICHARD J. KLARES ‖ PETER A. KLEIN ‖ ALAN D. KLEINBERG ‖ K
TRICIA KURAS ‖ NAUKA KUSHITANI ✠FF. THOMAS JOSEPH KUVEIKIS ‖ VICTOR KWARKYE ‖ KUI FAI KWOK ‖ ANGELA R. KYTE ‖ AMARNAUTH LACHHMAN
HEILA LAPIN ‖ CAROL ANN LAPLANTE ‖ INGEBORG ASTRID DESIREE LARIBY ‖ ROBIN LARKEY ‖ CHRISTOPHER RANDALL LARRABEE ‖ HAMIDOU S. LAR
S LEDUC ‖ HYUN-JOON 'PAUL' LEE ‖ JONG-MIN LEE ‖ MYUNG-WOO LEE ‖ DAVID S. LEE ‖ GARY H. LEE ‖ JUANITA LEE ‖ LORRAINE LEE ‖ RICHARD Y.C
J. LEWIS ‖ MARGARET SUSAN LEWIS ‖ YE WEI LIANG ‖ ORASRI LIANGTHANASARN ✠FF. DANIEL F. LIBRETTI ‖ JOSEPH M. LICCIARDI ‖ EDWARD LICH
‖ SALVATORE P. LOPES ‖ LUIS LOPEZ ‖ DANIEL LOPEZ ‖ MANUEL L. LOPEZ ‖ GEORGE LOPEZ ‖ JOSEPH LOSTRANGIO ‖ CHET LOUIE ‖ STUART SEE
LYNCH ‖ ROBERT H. LYNCH ‖ SEAN PATRICK LYNCH ‖ SEAN LYNCH ✠FF. MICHAEL J. LYONS ✠LT. PATRICK J. LYONS ‖ MONICA LYONS ‖ ROBERT FRA
OSEPH E. MALONEY ‖ GENE E. MALOY ‖ CHRISTIAN MALTBY ‖ FRANCISCO MIGUEL 'FRANK' MANCINI ‖ JOSEPH MANGANO ‖ SARA ELIZABETH MANLEY
BERT GABRIEL MARTINEZ ‖ LIZIE MARTINEZ-CALDERON ✠LT. PAUL RICHARD MARTINI ✠FF. JOSEPH A. MASCALI ‖ BERNARD MASCARENHAS ‖ STEP
MBAYA ‖ JAMES J. MCALARY JR. ✠FF. BRIAN G. MCALEESE ‖ PATRICIA A. MCANENEY ‖ COLIN RICHARD MCARTHUR ✠FF. JOHN K. MCAVOY ‖ KE
AM E. MCGINN ‖ THOMAS HENRY MCGINNIS ‖ MICHAEL GREGORY MCGINTY ‖ ANN MCGOVERN ‖ SCOTT MARTIN MCGOVERN ✠BAT. CHIEF WILLIAM
MCNEIL ‖ JASELLINY MCNISH ‖ SEAN PETER MCNULTY ‖ CHRISTINE SHEILA MCNULTY ✠FF. ROBERT WILLIAM MCPADDEN ✠FF. TERENCE A. MCSHANE
GER ‖ GEORGE C. MERINO ✠EMT YAMEL MERINO ‖ GEORGE MERKOURIS ‖ DEBORAH MERRICK ‖ RAYMOND J. METZ ‖ JILL A. METZLER ‖ DAVID ROBERT
WILBERT MIRAILLE ‖ DOMENICK MIRCOVICH ‖ RAJESH A. MIRPURI ‖ JOSEPH MISTRULLI ‖ SUSAN MISZKOWICZ ✠LT. PAUL THOMAS MITCHELL ‖ RICHA
MORALES ‖ LUIS MORALES ✠BAT. CHIEF JOHN M. MORAN ‖ JOHN CHRISTOPHER MORAN ‖ KATHLEEN MORAN ‖ LINDSAY S. MOREHOUSE ‖ GEORGE
HEN V. MULDERRY ✠FF. RICHARD T. MULDOWNEY, JR. ✠FF. MICHAEL DERMOTT MULLAN ✠FF. DENNIS MICHAEL MULLIGAN ‖ PETER JAMES MULLIGA
MURRAY ‖ RICHARD TODD MYHRE ✠LT. ROBERT B. NAGEL ‖ TAKUYA NAKAMURA ‖ ALEXANDER J.R. NAPIER ‖ FRANK JOSEPH NAPLES ✠LT. JOHN P
IN NIEDERER ✠PO. ALFONSE J. NIEDERMEYER ‖ FRANK JOHN NIESTADT ‖ GLORIA NIEVES ‖ JUAN NIEVES ‖ TROY EDWARD NILSEN ‖ PAUL R. NIMBLE
RTY ✠FF. DOUGLAS E. OELSCHLAGER ‖ TAKASHI OGAWA ‖ ALBERT OGLETREE ‖ PHILIP PAUL OGNIBENE ‖ JAMES ANDREW O'GRADY ✠FF. JOSEPH JA
R ORGIELEWICZ ‖ MARGARET ORLOSKE ‖ VIRGINIA A. ORMISTON ✠FF. KEVIN M. O'ROURKE ‖ JUAN ROMERO OROZCO ‖ RONALD ORSINI ‖ PETER K. O
HARD 'RICO' PALAZZOLO ✠DEP. CHIEF ORIO JOSEPH PALMER ✠FF. FRANK A. PALOMBO ‖ ALAN N. PALUMBO ‖ CHRISTOPHER M. PANATIER ‖ DOMINIC
UMA JR. ‖ JERROLD H. PASKINS ‖ HORACE ROBERT PASSANANTI ‖ SUZANNE H. PASSARO ‖ VICTOR ANTONIO MARTINEZ PASTRANA ‖ MANISH K. PATEL ‖
JON A. PERCONTI ‖ ALEJO PEREZ ‖ ANGEL PEREZ ‖ ANGELA SUSAN PEREZ ‖ IVAN PEREZ ‖ NANCY E. PEREZ ‖ ANTHONY PERFETTO ‖ JOSEPH JOHN PERR
IS J. PIERCE ‖ JOSEPH A. DELLA PIETRA ‖ BERNARD T. PIETRONICO ‖ NICHOLAS P. PIETRUNTI ‖ THEODOROS PIGIS ‖ SUSAN ELIZABETH ANCONA PIN
VIN M. PRIOR ‖ EVERETT MARTIN 'MARTY' PROCTOR ‖ CARRIE B. PROGEN ‖ DAVID LEE PRUIM ✠BAT. CHIEF RICHARD A. PRUNTY ‖ JOHN F. PUCKETT ‖
S 'LUKE' RAMBOUSEK ‖ JULIO FERNANDEZ RAMIREZ ‖ MARIA ISABEL RAMIREZ ‖ HARRY RAMOS ‖ VISHNOO RAMSAROOP ‖ LORENZO RAMZEY ‖ A. TOD
ILLY ‖ JAMES BRIAN REILLY ‖ TIMOTHY E. REILLY ‖ JOSEPH REINA ‖ THOMAS BARNES REINIG ‖ FRANK B. REISMAN ‖ JOSHUA SCOTT REISS ‖ KAREN
MOISES N. RIVAS ✠FF. JOSEPH RIVELLI, JR. ‖ ISAIAS RIVERA ‖ LINDA RIVERA ‖ JUAN WILLIAM RIVERA ‖ CARMEN A. RIVERA ‖ DAVID E. RIVERS ‖ JOSE
ORY E. RODRIGUEZ ‖ DAVID B. RODRIGUEZ-VARGAS ✠FF. MATTHEW S. ROGAN ‖ KARLIE BARBARA ROGERS ‖ SCOTT ROHNER ✠FF. KEITH ROMA ‖ JOS
DONNA MARIE ROTHENBERG ‖ NICK ROWE ✠SGT. TIMOTHY A. ROY ✠FF. PAUL G. RUBACK ‖ RONALD J. RUBEN ‖ JOANNE RUBINO ‖ DAVID MICHAEL R
OEL SAFRONOFF ‖ EDWARD SAIYA ‖ JOHN PATRICK SALAMONE ‖ HERNANDO R. SALAS ‖ JUAN SALAS ‖ ESMERLIN SALCEDO ‖ JOHN SALVATORE SALE
T MARIO L. SANTORO ‖ RAFAEL HUMBERTO SANTOS ‖ RUFINO CONRADO F. 'ROY' SANTOS ‖ KALYAN K. SARKAR ‖ CHAPELLE SARKER ‖ PAUL F. SARLE ‖
IER ‖ JOHN T. SCHROEDER ‖ SUSAN LEE KENNEDY SCHULER ‖ EDWARD W. SCHUNK ‖ MARK E. SCHURMEIER ‖ CLARIN SHELLIE SCHWARTZ ‖ JOHN SCHW
MOHAMMED SHAJAHAN ‖ GARY SHAMAY ‖ EARL RICHARD SHANAHAN ‖ SHIV SHANKAR ‖ NEIL G. SHASTRI ‖ KATHRYN ANNE SHATZOFF ‖ BARBARA
RY SIMOWITZ ✠EMT JEFF L. SIMPSON ‖ ROSHAN R. 'SEAN' SINGH ‖ KHAMLADAI K. 'KHAMI' SINGH ‖ THOMAS E. SINTON ‖ PETER A. SIRACUSE ‖ SIRIUS
NIE S. SMITHWICK ‖ ROCHELLE MONIQUE SNELL ‖ LEONARD J. SNYDER ‖ ASTRID ELIZABETH SOHAN ‖ SUSHIL SOLANKI ‖ RUBEN SOLARES ‖ NAOMI
ES STADELBERGER ‖ ERIC A. STAHLMAN ✠FF. GREGORY M. STAJK ‖ CORINA STAN ‖ ALEXANDRU LIVIU STAN ‖ MARY D. STANLEY ‖ JOYCE STANTON
USS ‖ STEVEN F. STROBERT ✠PO. WALWYN W. STUART ✠FF. BENJAMIN SUAREZ ‖ DAVID S. SUAREZ ✠PO. RAMON SUAREZ ‖ YOICHI SUGIYAMA ‖ WIL
ICHAEL TADDONIO ‖ KEIJI TAKAHASHI ‖ KEIICHIRO TAKAHASHI ‖ PHYLLIS GAIL TALBOT ‖ ROBERT R. TALHAMI ✠FF. SEAN PATRICK TALLON ✠PO. PAUL T
UMATIE T. THACKURDEEN ‖ HARSHAD SHAM THATTE ‖ THOMAS F. THEURKAUF ‖ LESLEY ANNE THOMAS ‖ BRIAN T. THOMPSON ‖ CLIVE THOMPSON ‖ G
HEN K. TOMPSETT ‖ THOMAS TONG ‖ AZUCENA DE LA TORRE ‖ DORIS TORRES ‖ LUIS EDUARDO TORRES ‖ AMY E. TOYEN ‖ CHRISTOPHER M. TRAINA ‖
N V. UPTON ‖ DIANE MARIA URBAN ‖ UNKNOWN ‖ JOHN DAMIEN VACCACIO ‖ BRADLEY H. VADAS ‖ WILLIAM VALCARCEL ‖ MAYRA VALDES-RODRIGUEZ
NNA ‖ ROBERT A. VICARIO ‖ CELESTE TORRES VICTORIA ‖ JOANNA VIDAL ✠FF. JOHN T. VIGIANO II ✠DET. JOSEPH VINCENT VIGIANO ‖ FRANK J. VIGNOL
ALLENDORF ‖ MATTHEW BLAKE WALLENS ‖ JOHN WALLICE ‖ BARBARA P. WALSH ‖ JAMES WALSH ✠LT. JEFFREY PATRICK WALZ ‖ CHING H. WANG ‖
S ✠FF. TIMOTHY MATTHEW WELTY ‖ CHRISTIAN HANS RUDOLF WEMMERS ‖ SSU-HUI 'VANESSA' WEN ‖ OLEH D. WENGERCHUK ‖ PETER M. WEST ‖ W
‖ KEVIN MICHAEL WILLIAMS ‖ LOUIS CALVIN WILLIAMS ‖ LOUIE ANTHONY WILLIAMS ✠BAT. CHIEF JOHN WILLIAMSON ‖ CYNTHIA WILSON ‖ DONNA W
ENTLEY WORKS ‖ MARTIN MICHAEL WORTLEY ‖ RODNEY JAMES WOTTON ✠FF. RET. WILLIAM WREN ‖ JOHN W. WRIGHT JR. ‖ NEIL R. WRIGHT ‖ SAND
ZEPLIN ‖ JIE YAO JUSTIN ZHAO ‖ IVELIN ZIMINSKI ‖ MICHAEL JOSEPH ZINZI ‖ CHARLES A. ZION ‖ JULIE LYNNE ZIPPER ‖ SALVATORE J. ZISA ‖ PROKOPIO
ERG ✠ DANA FALKENBERG ✠ JAMES JOE FERGUSON ✠ WILSON "BUD" FLAGG ✠ DARLENE FLAGG ✠ RICHARD GABRIEL ✠ IAN J. GRAY ✠ STANLEY H
KI YANCEY ✠ SHUYIN YANG ✠ YUGUAG ZHEN ○ PENTAGON ○ SPC. CRAIG AMUNDSON ○ MELISSA ROSE BARNES ○ 'RETIRED' MASTER SGT. MAX BEILKE
PATRICK S. DUNN ○ EDWARD THOMAS EARHART ○ LT. CMDR. ROBERT RANDOLPH ELSETH ○ JAMIE LYNN FALLON ○ AMELIA V. FIELDS ○ GERALD P. FISH
TBOURN-ALLEN ○ MAJ. STEVE LONG ○ JAMES LYNCH ○ TERENCE M. LYNCH ○ NEHAMON LYONS ○ SHELLEY A. MARSHALL ○ TERESA MARTIN ○ ADA L. M
MSAUR ○ RHONDA RASMUSSEN ○ MARSHA DIANAH RATCHFORD ○ MARTHA RESZKE ○ CECELIA E. RICHARD ○ EDWARD V. ROWENHORST ○ JUDY ROWLE
LBERT ○ WILLIE Q. TROY ○ LT. CMDR. RONALD JAMES VAUK ○ LT. COL. KAREN WAGNER ○ META L. WALLER ○ STAFF SGT. MAUDLYN A. WHITE ○ SANDRA

2977 INNOCENT LIVES LO

CHARLES JENKINS ✠ CHARLES EDWARD JONES ✠ BARBARA KEATING ✠ DAVID KOVALCIN ✠ JUDY LAROCQUE ✠ NATALIE JANIS LASDEN ✠ DANIEL JOHN LEE ✠ DA
JUAREZ ✠ MICHAEL THEODORIDIS ✠ JAMES TRENTINI ✠ MARY TRENTINI ✠ PENDYALA VAMSIKRISHNA ✠ MARY WAHLSTROM ✠ KENNETH WALDIE ✠ JOHN WEN
EIJEN ✠ JOHN 'JAY' J. CORCORAN ✠ DOROTHY ALMA DEARAUJO ✠ ANA GLORIA POCASANGRE DE BARRERA ✠ LISA FROST ✠ RONALD GAMBOA ✠ LYNN CATH
H MAGDALINE MCCOURT ✠ WOLFGANG PETER MENZEL ✠ SHAWN M. NASSANEY ✠ MARIE PAPPALARDO ✠ PATRICK QUIGLEY ✠ FREDERICK CHARLES RIMM
A ADAMS ‖ STEPHEN ADAMS ‖ PATRICK ADAMS ‖ IGNATIUS ADANGA ‖ CHRISTY A. ADDAMO ‖ TERENCE E. ADDERLEY ‖ SOPHIA B. ADDO ‖ LEE ADLER ‖ DANIEL
RETTO ✠FF. ERIC ALLEN ‖ JOSEPH RYAN ALLEN ‖ RICHARD LANARD ALLEN ✠FF. RICHARD DENNIS ALLEN ‖ CHRISTOPHER EDWARD ALLINGHAM ‖ JANET M
A ANGILLETTA ‖ DOREEN J. ANGRISANI ‖ LORRAINE D. ANTIGUA ‖ PETER PAUL APOLLO ✠FF. FAUSTINO APOSTOL JR. ‖ FRANK THOMAS AQUILINO ‖ PATRICK M
'RUDY' BACCHUS ‖ JOHN JAMES BADAGLIACCA ‖ JANE ELLEN BAESZLER ‖ ROBERT J. BAIERWALTER ‖ ANDREW J. BAILEY ‖ BRETT T. BAILEY ‖ TATYANA BA
BARZVI ‖ INNA BASINA ‖ ALYSIA BASMAJIAN ‖ KENNETH WILLIAM BASNICKI ✠LT. STEVEN J. BATES ‖ PAUL JAMES BATTAGLIA ‖ W. DAVID BAUER ‖ IVHAN LU
GER ‖ STEVEN HOWARD BERGER ✠FF. JOHN P. BERGIN ‖ ALVIN BERGSOHN ‖ DANIEL D. BERGSTEIN ‖ MICHAEL J. BERKELEY ‖ DONNA BERNAERTS-KEARNS ‖ D
NICE L. BLANEY ‖ CRAIG MICHAEL BLASS ‖ RITA BLAU ‖ RICHARD M. BLOOD ‖ MICHAEL A. BOCCARDI ‖ JOHN PAUL BOCCHI ✠FF. MICHAEL L. BOCCHINO ‖ SUSA
BOWMAN ‖ SHAWN EDWARD BOWMAN ‖ KEVIN L. BOWSER ✠FF. GARY R. BOX ‖ GENNADY BOYARSKY ‖ PAMELA BOYCE ✠FF. MICHAEL BOYLE ‖ ALFRED BRACA ‖
FER ‖ KEITH BROOMFIELD ‖ JANICE J. BROWN ‖ LLOYD BROWN ✠CAPT. PATRICK J. BROWN ‖ BETTINA BROWNE ‖ MARK BRUCE ‖ RICHARD BRUEHERT ✠FF. ANDR
LILLIAN CACERES ‖ BRIAN JOSEPH CACHIA ‖ STEVEN CAFIERO ‖ RICHARD M. CAGGIANO ‖ CECILE M. CAGUICLA ‖ MICHAEL JOHN CAHILL ‖ SCOTT W. CAHILL
OSI ‖ STEPHEN J. CANGIALOSI ‖ LISA B. CANNAVA ✠FF. BRIAN CANNIZZARO ‖ MICHAEL R. CANTY ‖ LOUIS A. CAPORICCI ‖ JONATHAN N. CAPPELLO ‖ JAMES CHR
CASPAR ‖ ALEJANDRO CASTANO ‖ ARCELIA CASTILLO ‖ LEONARD M. CASTRIANNO ‖ JOSE RAMON CASTRO ‖ RICHARD G. CATARELLI ‖ CHRISTOPHER SEAN C
✠FF. VERNON PAUL CHERRY ‖ NESTOR CHEVALIER ‖ SWEDE JOSEPH CHEVALIER ‖ ALEXANDER H. CHIANG ‖ DOROTHY J. CHIARCHIARO ‖ LUIS ALFONSO CH
NNIE LEROY CLARK ‖ THOMAS R. CLARK ‖ EUGENE CLARK ‖ BENJAMIN KEEFE CLARK ‖ CHRISTOPHER ROBERT CLARKE ‖ DONNA CLARKE ✠FF. MICHAEL J. CLA
N ‖ ROBERT D. COLIN ‖ ROBERT J. COLL ‖ JEAN MARIE COLLIN ✠FF. JOHN MICHAEL COLLINS ‖ MICHAEL L. COLLINS ‖ THOMAS J. COLLINS ‖ JOSEPH COLLISO
EN D. CORREA ‖ DANNY A. CORREA-GUTIERREZ ✠CAPT. JAMES J. CORRIGAN ‖ CARLOS CORTES ‖ KEVIN M. COSGROVE ‖ DOLORES MARIE COSTA ‖ DIGNA ALEX
C CROSS ‖ HELEN CROSSIN-KITTLE ‖ KEVIN RAYMOND CROTTY ‖ THOMAS G. CROTTY ‖ JOHN CROWE ‖ WELLES REMY CROWTHER ‖ ROBERT L. CRUIKSHANK ‖
OS ‖ JACK L. D'AMBROSI ‖ JEANNINE MARIE DAMIANI-JONES ‖ PATRICK W. DANAHY ‖ NANA KWUKU DANSO ‖ MARY D'ANTONIO PO. VINCENT G. DANZ ‖
‖ JAMES VINCENT DEBLASE ‖ PAUL DECOLA ‖ SIMON DEDVUKAJ ‖ JASON CHRISTOPHER DEFAZIO ‖ DAVID A. DEFEO ‖ JENNIFER DE JESUS ‖ MONIQUE E. DE
‖ CINDY ANN DEUEL ‖ JERRY DEVITO ‖ ROBERT P. DEVITT ✠BAT. CHIEF DENNIS LAWRENCE DEVLIN ✠FF. GERARD P. JERRY DEWAN ‖ SIMON SULEMAN ALI DI
DOUGLAS FRANK DISTEFANO ‖ RAMZI A. DOANY ‖ JOHN J. DOHERTY ‖ MELISSA C. DOI ‖ BRENDAN DOLAN ‖ NEIL DOLLARD ‖ JAMES JOSEPH DOMANIC
GIGER ‖ JACKIE SAYEGH DUGGAN ‖ SAREVE DUKAT ‖ CHRISTOPHER JOSEPH DUNNE ‖ RICHARD A. DUNSTAN ‖ PATRICK THOMAS DWYER ‖ JOSEPH ANTHONY E
‖ EDGAR H. EMERY ‖ DORIS SUK-YUEN ENG ‖ CHRISTOPHER S. EPPS ‖ ULF RAMM ERICSON ‖ ERWIN L. ERKER ‖ WILLIAM J. ERWIN ‖ SARAH 'ALI' ESCARCEGA
FARLEY ‖ ELIZABETH ANN 'BETTY' FARMER ‖ DOUGLAS FARNUM ‖ JOHN W. FARRELL ✠FF. TERRENCE PATRICK FARRELL ‖ JOHN G. FARRELL ✠BAT. CHIEF JO
LLERIN FERREIRA ‖ ROBERT JOHN FERRIS ‖ DAVID FRANCIS FERRUGIO ‖ LOUIS V. FERSINI ‖ MICHAEL DAVID FERUGIO ‖ BRADLEY JAMES FETCHET ‖ JENNIFE
FLICKINGER ✠FF. JOHN JOSEPH FLORIO ‖ JOSEPH W. FLOUNDERS ‖ DAVID FODOR ✠LT. MICHAEL N. FODOR ‖ STEVEN MARK FOGEL ✠FF. THOMAS J. FOLEY
FREIMAN ✠LT. PETER L. FREUND ‖ ARLENE E. FRIED ‖ ALAN WAYNE FRIEDLANDER ‖ ANDREW K. FRIEDMAN PO. GREGG J. FROEHNER ‖ PETER C.
AR GARCIA ‖ DAVID GARCIA ‖ JORGE LUIS MORRON GARCIA ‖ JUAN GARCIA ‖ MARLYN C. GARCIA ‖ CHRISTOPHER GARDNER ‖ DOUGLAS B. GARDNER
ANNE GERATY ‖ RALPH GERHARDT ‖ ROBERT J. GERLICH ✠FF. DENIS P. GERMAIN ‖ MARINA R. GERTSBERG ‖ SUSAN M. GETZENDANNER ‖ JAMES GE
GIUGLIANO ‖ MON GJONBALAJ ‖ DIANNE GLADSTONE ✠FF. KEITH ALEXANDER GLASCOE ‖ THOMAS I. GLASSER ‖ HARRY GLENN ‖ BARRY H. GLICK ‖
GORDON ‖ SEBASTIAN GORKI ‖ KIERAN GORMAN PO. THOMAS E. GORMAN ‖ MICHAEL EDWARD GOULD ‖ YUGI GOYA ‖ JON RICHARD GRABOWSKI ‖ C
JOHN M. GRIFFIN ‖ TAWANNA GRIFFIN ‖ JOAN D. GRIFFITH ‖ WARREN GRIFKA ‖ RAMON GRIJALVO ‖ JOSEPH F. GRILLO ‖ DAVID GRIMNER ‖ KENNETH
ALE ‖ RICHARD HALL ‖ VASWALD GEORGE HALL ‖ ROBERT JOHN HALLIGAN ✠LT. VINCENT GERARD HALLORAN ‖ JAMES D. HALVORSON EMT MOHAMMAD
RICK HART ‖ JOHN CLINTON HARTZ ‖ EMERIC J. HARVEY ✠BAT. CHIEF THOMAS T. HASKELL ✠FF. TIMOTHY S. HASKELL ‖ JOSEPH JOHN HASSON ✠CAPT. TER
P. HENRY ✠FF. WILLIAM L. HENRY ‖ JOHN HENWOOD ‖ ROBERT ALLAN HEPBURN ‖ MARY 'MOLLY' HERENCIA ‖ LINDSAY COATES HERKNESS ‖ HARVEY RO
STEPHEN G. HOFFMAN ‖ MARCIA HOFFMAN ‖ FREDERICK J. HOFFMANN ‖ MICHELE L. HOFFMANN ‖ JUDITH FLORENCE HOFMILLER ‖ THOMAS WARREN HOHLWEC
‖ THOMAS F. HUGHES ‖ TIMOTHY ROBERT HUGHES ‖ PAUL R. HUGHES ‖ ROBERT T. "BOBBY" HUGHES ‖ SUSAN HUIE ‖ MYCHAL LAMAR HULSE ‖ WILLIAM C. HUNT
IVANTSOV ‖ VIRGINIA JABLONSKI ‖ BROOKE ALEXANDRA JACKMAN ‖ AARON JACOBS ‖ JASON KYLE JACOBS ‖ MICHAEL GRADY JACOBS ‖ ARIEL LOUIS JACO
RSTMANN JONES ‖ BRIAN L. JONES ‖ CHRISTOPHER D. JONES ‖ DONALD T. JONES ‖ DONALD W. JONES ‖ LINDA JONES ‖ MARY S. JONES ✠FF. ANDREW B.
R. KANTER ‖ DEBORAH H. KAPLAN ‖ ALVIN PETER KAPPELMANN ‖ CHARLES KARCZEWSKI ‖ WILLIAM A. KARNES ‖ DOUGLAS G. KARPILOFF ✠DEP. CHIEF
‖ TIMOTHY C. KELLY ‖ WILLIAM HILL KELLY ‖ ROBERT C. KENNEDY ✠FF. THOMAS J. KENNEDY ‖ JOHN KEOHANE ‖ LT. RONALD T. KERWIN ‖ HOWARD L. KES
R RONALD PHILIP KLOEPFER ‖ YEVGENY KNIAZEV ‖ THOMAS PATRICK KNOX ‖ ANDREW KNOX ‖ REBECCA LEE KOBORIE ‖ DEBORAH KOBUS ‖ GARY EDWARD KO
GANESH LADKAT ‖ JAMES P. LADLEY ‖ DANIEL M. VAN LAERE ‖ JOSEPH A. LAFALCE ‖ JEANETTE LAFOND-MENICHINO ✠FF. DAVID J. LAFORGE ‖ MICHAEL PAT
‖ JOHN ADAM LARSON ‖ GARY E. LASKO ‖ NICHOLAS C. LASSMAN PO. PAUL LASZCZYNSKI ‖ JEFFREY LATOUCHE ‖ CRISTINA DE LAURA ‖ OSCAR DE LAUR
KATHRYN BLAIR LEE ‖ STUART 'SOO-JIN' LEE ‖ LINDA C. LEE ‖ STEPHEN LEFKOWITZ ‖ ADRIANA LEGRO ‖ EDWARD J. LEHMAN ‖ ERIC ANDREW LEHRFELD ‖ D
✠EMT CARLOS R. LILLO ‖ CRAIG DAMIAN LILORE ‖ ARNOLD A. LIM ‖ DARYA LIN ‖ WEI RONG LIN ‖ NICKIE L. LINDO ‖ THOMAS V. LINEHAN ✠FF. R
MICHAEL W. LOWE ‖ GARRY LOZIER ‖ JOHN PETER LOZOWSKY ‖ CHARLES PETER LUCANIA ‖ EDWARD 'TED' H. LUCKETT ‖ MARK G. LUDVIGSEN ‖ LEE CH
‖ CATHERINE FAIRFAX MACRAE ‖ RICHARD B. MADDEN ‖ SIMON MADDISON ‖ NOELL MAERZ ‖ JEANNIEANN MAFFEO ✠FF. JOSEPH MAFFEO ‖ JAY RO
‖ TERENCE J. MANNING ‖ MARION VICTORIA 'VICKIE' MANNING ‖ JAMES MAOUNIS ✠DEP. CHIEF JOSEPH ROSS MARCHBANKS ‖ PETER EDWARD MARDIKIAN ‖ E
G. MASSA ‖ PATRICIA A. CIMAROLI MASSARI ‖ MICHAEL MASSAROLI ‖ PHILIP W. MASTRANDREA ‖ RUDOLPH MASTROCINQUE ‖ JOSEPH MATHAI ‖ CHARLES
BRENDAN MCCABE ‖ MICHAEL J. MCCABE ✠FF. THOMAS J. MCCANN ‖ JUSTIN MCCARTHY ‖ KEVIN M. MCCARTHY ‖ MICHAEL DESMOND MCCARTHY ‖ ROBE
S. MCGOWAN ‖ FRANCIS NOEL MCGUINN ‖ PATRICK J. MCGUIRE ‖ THOMAS M. MCHALE ‖ KEITH MCHEFFEY ‖ DENNIS J. MCHUGH ✠FF. DENNIS P. MCHUGH ‖
MCSWEENEY ✠FF. MARTIN E. MCWILLIAMS ‖ ROCCO A. MEDAGLIA ‖ ABIGAIL MEDINA ‖ ANA IRIS MEDINA ‖ DEBORAH MEDWIG ‖ WILLIAM J. MEEHAN ‖ DAMIAN
IAH ‖ WILLIAM EDWARD MICCIULLI ‖ MARTIN PAUL MICHELSTEIN ‖ LUIS CLODOALDO REVILLA MIER ‖ PETER T. MILANO ‖ GREGORY MILANOWYCZ ‖ LUKASZ T. M
MOCCIA ✠BAT. CHIEF LOUIS JOSEPH MODAFFERI ‖ BOYIE MOHAMMED ✠LT. DENNIS MOJICA ✠FF. MANUEL MOJICA JR. ‖ MANUEL DEJESUS MOLINA ‖ FERNAN
RELLO ✠FF. VINCENT S. MORELLO ‖ ARTURO ALVA MORENO ‖ YVETTE NICOLE MORENO ‖ DOROTHY MORGAN ‖ RICHARD MORGAN ‖ NANCY MORGENSTERN ‖ S
LIN ‖ JAMES DONALD MUNHALL ‖ NANCY MUNIZ ‖ CARLOS MARIO MUNOZ ‖ FRANCISCO HELADIO MU–OZ ‖ THERESA 'TERRY' MUNSON ‖ ROBERT M. MURAC
A. NARDELLA ‖ MARIO NARDONE ‖ MANIKA NARULA ‖ NARENDER NATH ‖ KAREN S. NAVARRO PO. JOSEPH M. NAVAS ‖ FRANCIS J. NAZARIO ‖ GLENRO
VIVEN ‖ KATHERINE 'KATIE' MCGARRY NOACK ‖ CURTIS TERRENCE NOEL ‖ DANIEL R. NOLAN ‖ ROBERT WALTER NOONAN ‖ DANIELA R. NOTARO ‖ BRIAN C. NO
G. O'HAGAN ✠FF. SAMUEL P. OITICE ✠FF. PATRICK O'KEEFE ✠CAPT. WILLIAM S. O'KEEFE ‖ GERALD MICHAEL OLCOTT ‖ GERALD O'LEARY ‖ CHRISTINE ANNE
ORTIZ ‖ DAVID ORTIZ ‖ PAUL ORTIZ ‖ SONIA ORTIZ ‖ ALEXANDER ORTIZ ‖ PABLO ORTIZ ‖ MASARU OSE ‖ ROBERT W. O'SHEA ‖ PATRICK J. O'SHEA ‖ JAMES RO
ARSHALL PAUL J. PANSINI ✠DEP. CHIEF JOHN M. PAOLILLO ‖ EDWARD J. PAPA ‖ SALVATORE T. PAPASSO ✠FF. JAMES N. PAPPAGEORGE ‖ VINOD K. PARAKAT ‖
EL ‖ DIPTI PATEL ‖ STEVEN B. PATERSON ‖ JAMES MATTHEW PATRICK ‖ MANUEL PATROCINO ‖ BERNARD E. PATTERSON ‖ CIRA MARIE PATTI ‖ ROBERT EDWARD
RROTTA ✠LT. GLENN C. PERRY ‖ EMELDA PERRY PO. JOHN WILLIAM PERRY ‖ FRANKLIN ALLAN PERSHEP ‖ DANIEL PESCE ‖ MICHAEL J. PESCHERINE ‖ DAVI
‖ CHRISTOPHER TODD PITMAN ‖ JOSH MICHAEL PIVER ‖ JOSEPH PLUMITALLO ‖ JOHN M. POCHER ‖ WILLIAM HOWARD POHLMANN ‖ LAURENCE M. POLATSCH
EDWARD F. PULLIS ‖ PATRICIA ANN PUMA ‖ HEMANTH KUMAR PUTTUR ‖ EDWARD R. PYKON ‖ CHRISTOPHER QUACKENBUSH ‖ LARS PETER QUALBEN ✠FF. LIN
VID RAND ‖ JONATHAN C. RANDALL ‖ SRINIVASA SHREYAS RANGANATH ‖ ANNE ROSE T. RANSOM ‖ FAINA RAPOPORT ‖ ROBERT ARTHUR RASMUSSEN ‖ AME
D REO ‖ RICHARD RESCORLA ‖ JOHN THOMAS RESTA ‖ SYLVIA SAN PIO RESTA ‖ EDUVIGIS 'EDDIE' REYES PO. BRUCE A. REYNOLDS ‖ JOHN FREDERICK RH
ZZA ‖ JOHN FRANK RIZZO ‖ STEPHEN LOUIS ROACH ‖ JOSEPH ROBERTO ‖ LEO A. ROBERTS ✠FF. MICHAEL E. ROBERTS ✠FF. MICHAEL EDWARD ROBERTS ‖ DO
VIN SANTIAGO ROMERO ‖ EFRAIN FRANCO ROMERO CHIEF JAMES A. ROMITO ‖ SEAN ROONEY ‖ ERIC THOMAS ROPITEAU ‖ AIDA ROSARIO ‖ ANGELA ROSAR
UGGIERE ‖ SUSAN ANN RUGGIERO ‖ ADAM K. RUHALTER ‖ GILBERT RUIZ ✠FF. STEPHEN P. RUSSELL ‖ STEVEN HARRIS RUSSIN ✠LT. MICHAEL THOMAS RUSS
ARDI ‖ WAYNE JOHN SALOMAN ‖ NOLBERT SALOMON ‖ CATHERINE PATRICIA SALTER ‖ FRANK SALVATERRA ‖ PAUL R. SALVIO ‖ SAMUEL R. SALVO ‖ CARLOS
RI ✠FF. GREGORY THOMAS SAUCEDO ‖ SUE SAUER ‖ ANTHONY SAVAS ‖ VLADIMIR SAVINKIN ‖ JOHN SBARBARO ‖ ROBERT L. SCANDOLE ‖ MICHELLE SCARPITTA ‖
ARTZ ‖ ADRIANE VICTORIA SCIBETTA ‖ RAPHAEL SCORCA ‖ RANDOLPH SCOTT ‖ CHRISTOPHER J. SCUDDER ‖ ARTHUR WARREN SCULLIN ‖ MICHAEL SEAMAN ‖
AW ‖ ROBERT J. SHAY ‖ DANIEL JAMES SHEA ‖ JOSEPH PATRICK SHEA ‖ LINDA J. SHEEHAN ‖ HAGAY SHEFI ‖ JOHN ANTHONY SHERRY ‖ ATSUSHI SHIRATOR
LOS ‖ JOSEPH M. SISOLAK PO. JOHN P. SKALA ‖ FRANCIS J. SKIDMORE ‖ TOYENA CORLISS SKINNER ‖ PAUL ALBERT SKRZYPEK ‖ CHRISTOPHER PAUL SLATT
EL W. SONS ‖ MICHAEL C. SORRESSE ‖ FABIAN SOTO ‖ TIMOTHY P. SOULAS ‖ GREGORY T. SPAGNOLETTI ‖ DONALD F. SPAMPINATO JR. ‖ THOMAS SPARACIO
ANTHONY M. STARITA ✠FF. JEFFREY STARK ‖ DEREK JAMES STATKEVICUS ‖ CRAIG WILLIAM STAUB ‖ WILLIAM V. STECKMAN ‖ ERIC THOMAS STEEN ‖ WILL
RA ✠FF. DANIEL T. SUHR ✠EMT DAVID MARC SULLINS ✠LT. CHRISTOPHER P. SULLIVAN ‖ PATRICK SULLIVAN ‖ THOMAS SULLIVAN ‖ HILARIO SORIANO 'LARRY
ACHEL TAMARES ‖ HECTOR TAMAYO ‖ MICHAEL ANDREW TAMUCCIO ‖ KENICHIRO TANAKA ‖ RHONDELLE CHERIE TANKARD ‖ MICHAEL ANTHONY TANNER ‖ DE
ANTHONY THOMPSON ‖ VANAVAH ALEXI THOMPSON CAPT. WILLIAM HARRY THOMPSON ‖ NIGEL BRUCE THOMPSON ‖ ERIC RAYMOND THORPE ‖ NICHOLA A.
A ABDOUL KARIM TRAORE ‖ WALTER 'WALLY' P. TRAVERS ‖ GLENN J. TRAVERS ‖ FELICIA TRAYLOR-BASS ‖ LISA L. TREROTOLA ‖ KARAMO TRERRA ‖ MICHAEL
VAN VALE PO. SANTOS VALENTIN ‖ BENITO VALENTIN ‖ CARLTON FRANCIS VALVO ‖ EDWARD RAYMOND VANACORE ‖ JON C. VANDEVANDER ✠FF. RICHARD BR
✠FF. SERGIO VILLANUEVA ‖ CHANTAL VINCELLI ‖ MELISSA VINCENT ‖ FRANCINE A. VIRGILIO ✠FF. LAWRENCE J. VIRGILIO ‖ JOSEPH G. VISCIANO ‖ JOSHUA S. VIT
HAEL P. WARCHOLA ‖ STEPHEN GORDON WARD ‖ JAMES A. WARING ‖ BRIAN G. WARNER ‖ DERRICK WASHINGTON ‖ CHARLES WATERS ‖ JAMES THOMAS 'MU
DITH LYNN WHALEN ✠FF. EUGENE M. WHELAN ‖ JOHN S. WHITE ✠FF. EDWARD JAMES WHITE ‖ JAMES PATRICK WHITE ‖ KENNETH W. WHITE ‖ LEONARD A.
ON ‖ DAVID H. WINTON ‖ GLENN J. WINUK ‖ THOMAS FRANCIS WISE ‖ ALAN L. WISNIEWSKI ‖ FRANK T. WISNIEWSKI ‖ DAVID WISWALL ‖ SIGRID CHARLOTTE
MBEM ‖ SURESH YANAMADALA ‖ MATTHEW DAVID YARNELL ‖ MYRNA YASKULKA ‖ SHAKILA YASMIN ‖ OLABISI L. YEE ‖ EDWARD P. YORK ‖ KEVIN PATRICK YORK
ZUCCALA ‖ ANDREW STEVEN ZUCKER ‖ IGOR ZUKELMAN ✠ FLIGHT 77 ✠ CHARLES BURLINGAME ✠ DAVID M. CHARLEBOIS ✠ MICHELE HEIDENBERGER ✠ JENN
STEVEN D. JACOBY ✠ ANN JUDGE ✠ CHANDLER KELLER ✠ YVONNE KENNEDY ✠ NORMA KHAN ✠ KAREN A. KINCAID ✠ DONG LEE ✠ DORA MENCHACA ✠ CH
AT ○ CARRIE BLAGBURN ○ LT. COL. CANFIELD D. BOONE ○ DONNA BOWEN ○ ALLEN BOYLE ○ CHRISTOPHER LEE BURFORD ○ DANIEL MARTIN CABALLERO ○ S
L. FLOCCO ○ SANDRA N. FOSTER ○ CAPT. LAWRENCE DANIEL GETZFRED ○ CORTZ GHEE ○ BRENDA C. GIBSON ○ RON GOLINSKI ○ DIANE M. HALE-MCKINZY ○ CA
M MATTSON ○ LT. GEN. TIMOTHY J. MAUDE ○ ROBERT J. MAXWELL ○ MOLLY MCKENZIE ○ PATRICIA E. 'PATTI' MICKLEY ○ MAJ. RONALD D. MILAM ○ GERARD 'JERR
WILLIAM R. RUTH ○ CHARLES E. SABIN ○ MARJORIE C. SALAMONE ○ LT. COL. DAVID M. SCALES ○ CMDR. ROBERT ALLAN SCHLEGEL ○ JANICE SCOTT ○ MIC
ILLCHER ○ LT. CMDR. DAVID LUCIAN WILLIAMS ○ MAJ. DWAYNE WILLIAMS ○ MARVIN R. WOODS ○ KEVIN WAYNE YOKUM ○ DONALD MCARTHUR YOUNG ○ LISA L.

ON SEPTEMBER 11, 2001

N A. MACKAY ✈ CHRISTOPHER D. MELLO ✈ JEFFREY MLADENIK ✈ ANTONIO JESUS MONTOYA VALDES ✈ CARLOS ALBERTO MONTOYMONTOYA ✈ LAURA LEE L LEE
WILLIAMS ✈ CHRISTOPHER ZARBA ✈ FLIGHT 175 ✈ ROBERT FANGMAN ✈ MICHAEL R. HORROCKS ✈ AMY N. JARRET ✈ AMY R. KMY R. KING ✈ KATHRYN IRRYN
ETER MORGAN GOODRICH ✈ DOUGLAS A. GOWELL ✈ THE REV. FRANCIS E. GROGAN ✈ CARL MAX HAMMOND ✈ PETER HANSON ✈ SON ✈ SUE JUE KIM-HAN-I-HA
✈ JESUS SANCHEZ, JR. ✈ MARY KATHLEEN SHEARER ✈ ROBERT MICHAEL SHEARER ✈ JANE LOUISE SIMPKIN ✈ BRIAN D. SWEENSWEENEY ✈ TIMOTHY WAHY W
MMANUEL AKUAKWAH ‖ ALOK AGARWAL ‖ MUKUL AGARWALA ✠LT. JOSEPH AGNELLO ‖ DAVID SCOTT AGNES ‖ JOAO A. F. AGUIAR JFUIAR JR. ✠LT. BRIAN G. NN G.
ALVARADO ‖ ANTONIO JAVIER ALVAREZ ‖ TELMO ALVEAR ‖ CESAR A. ALVIAR ‖ TARIQ AMANULLAH ‖ ANGELO AMARANTO ✠BAT. CBAT. CHIEF JAMES M. A M.
DAVID GREGORY ARCE ‖ MICHAEL G. ARCZYNSKI ✠FF. LOUIS ARENA ‖ ADAM ARIAS ‖ MICHAEL J. ARMSTRONG ‖ JACK CHARLES ARCES ARON ‖ JOSHUA ARO A ARC
S. BAKSH ‖ SHARON BALKCOM ‖ MICHAEL ANDREW BANE ‖ KATHY BANTIS ✠FF. GERARD JEAN BAPTISTE ‖ WALTER BARAN ✠ASST. ✠ASST. CHIEF GERARD ARRD A
MARLYN C. BAUTISTA ‖ JASPER BAXTER ‖ MICHELE 'DU BERRY' BEALE ‖ PAUL F. BEATINI ‖ JANE S. BEATTY ‖ LARRY I. BECK ‖ MANET MANETTE MARIE BECKLECKL
D ‖ WILLIAM BERNSTEIN ‖ DAVID M. BERRAY ‖ DAVID S. BERRY ‖ JOSEPH J. BERRY ‖ WILLIAM REED BETHKE ‖ TIMOTHY D. BETTERLETTERLY ‖ EDWARD F. BEFF. B
CE DOUGLAS CHAPPY BOEHM ‖ MARY KATHERINE BOFFA ‖ NICHOLAS A. BOGDAN ‖ DARREN C. BOHAN ‖ LAWRENCE FRANCIS BOISSE BOISSEAU ‖ VINCENT M. TT M.
CE ✠FF. KEVIN H. BRACKEN ‖ DAVID BRIAN BRADY ‖ ALEXANDER BRAGINSKY ‖ NICHOLAS W. BRANDEMARTI ‖ MICHELLE RENEE BRAEE BRATTON ‖ PATRICE RRICE
VINCENT E. BRUNTON ‖ FIRE MARSHAL RONALD PAUL BUCCA ‖ BRANDON J. BUCHANAN ✠FF. GREG JOSEPH BUCK ‖ DENNIS BUCKLEBUCKLEY ‖ NANCY BUECHUECH
FF. GEORGE C. CAIN ✠FF. SALVATORE B. CALABRO ‖ JOSEPH M. CALANDRILLO ‖ PHILIP V. CALCAGNO ‖ EDWARD CALDERON ‖ KENN ‖ KENNETH MARCUS CLUS
RICHARD M. CAPRONI ‖ JOSE CARDONA ✠FF. DENNIS M. CAREY ‖ STEPHEN CAREY ‖ EDWARD CARLINO ✠FF. MICHAEL SCOTT CARLO ‖ CARLO ‖ DAVID G. CARLOARLO
FIELD ‖ MARY TERESA CAULFIELD ‖ JUDSON CAVALIER ✠FF. MICHAEL JOSEPH CAWLEY ‖ JASON D. CAYNE ‖ JUAN ARMANDO CEBALLCEBALLOS ‖ MARCIA G. G G.
WING WAI 'EDDIE' CHING ✠ NICHOLAS P. CHIOFALO ✠FF. JOHN G. CHIPURA ‖ PETER A. CHIRCHIRILLO ‖ CATHERINE E. CHIRLS ‖ KYLS ‖ KYUNG HEE 'CASEY' ASE'
E ‖ KEVIN FRANCIS CLEARY ‖ JAMES D. CLEERE ‖ GEOFFREY W. CLOUD ‖ SUSAN M. CLYNE ✠FF. STEVEN COAKLEY ‖ JEFFREY COALE COALE ‖ PATRICIA A. COA A. C
ODNER ‖ LINDA M. COLON ‖ SOLEDI COLON ‖ RONALD COMER ‖ JAIME CONCEPCION ‖ ALBERT CONDE ‖ DENEASE CONLEY ‖ SUSAN SUSAN CLANCY CONLODNNLO
ZA ‖ CHARLES GREGORY COSTELLO JR. ‖ MICHAEL SHAMUS COSTELLO ‖ CONROD K.H. COTTOY ‖ MARTIN COUGHLAN ✠SGT. JOHN GEOHN GERARD COUGHLINHLIN
ROBERT CRUZ ‖ KENNETH JOHN CUBAS ‖ RICHARD JOSEPH CUDINA ‖ NEIL JAMES CUDMORE ✠FF. THOMAS PATRICK CULLEN III ‖ JOSEPH III ‖ JOAN MCCONNELLNNEL
‖ ELIZABETH ANN DARLING ‖ ANNETTE ANDREA DATARAM ✠LT. EDWARD ALEXANDER D'ATRI ✠FF. MICHAEL D. D'AURIA ‖ LAWR ‖ LAWRENCE DAVIDSONDSO
S ‖ DONALD A. DELAPENHA ‖ VITO JOSEPH DELEO ‖ DANIELLE DELIE ‖ COLLEEN ANN DELOUGHERY ✠LT. MANUEL DEL VALLE, JR. ‖ FRANCIS ALBERTUEL DEEL D
AGOSTINO ‖ MATTHEW DIAZ ‖ NANCY DIAZ ‖ OBDULIO RUIZ DIAZ ‖ LOURDES GALLETTI DIAZ ‖ MICHAEL DIAZ-PIEDRA LLL ‖ JUDITH BELGUESE DIAZ-SIEDRA DDRA
DOMINGO ‖ CHARLES 'CARLOS' DOMINGUEZ ✠PO. GERONIMO MARK PATRICK DOMINGUEZ ✠LT. KEVIN W. DONNELLY ‖ JACQUELINE DONOVAN ‖ STNNELLNNEL
E EAGLESON ‖ ROBERT D. EATON ‖ DEAN P. EBERLING ‖ MARGARET RUTH ECHTERMANN ‖ PAUL ROBERT ECKNA ‖ CONSTANTINE 'GUS' ECONOMOS ‖ NA ‖ CAA ‖
NY M. ESPINOZA ✠FF. FRANCIS ESPOSITO ✠CAPT. MICHAEL A. ESPOSITO ‖ WILLIAM ESPOSITO ‖ BRIGETTE ANN ESPOSITO ‖ RUBEN ESQUILIN ‖ SADIEN ESP E ESP
AS P. FARRELLY ‖ SYED ABDUL FATHA ‖ CHRISTOPHER FAUGHNAN ‖ WENDY R. FAULKNER ‖ SHANNON M. FAVA ‖ BERNARD D. FAVUZZA ✠PO. ROBERA ‖ BE ‖ BE
STEN NICOLE FIEDEL ‖ SAMUEL FIELDS ‖ MICHAEL BRADLEY FINNEGAN ‖ TIMOTHY J. FINNERTY ‖ FRANK FIORE ✠FF. MICHAEL CURTIS FIORE ‖ STEPH ✠FF. ✠FF
‖ CHIH MIN 'DENNIS' FOO ‖ DEL ROSE FORBES-CHEATHAM ‖ GODWIN FORDE ✠PO. DONALD A. FOREMAN ‖ CHRISTOPHER HUGH FORSYTHE ‖ CLAUDHRISTORRIST
T FUMANDO ‖ STEVEN ELLIOT FURMAN ‖ PAUL JAMES FURMATO ‖ FREDRIC GABLER ‖ RICHARD S. GABRIELLE ‖ JAMES ANDREW GADIEL ‖ PAMELA GA JAMEJAME
✠FF. THOMAS A. GARDNER ‖ JEFFREY B. GARDNER ‖ WILLIAM ARTHUR GARDNER ‖ FRANCESCO GARFI ‖ ROCCO GARGANO ‖ JAMES M. GARTENBERG ‖ O GARCGAR
M. GIACCONE ✠CAPT. VINCENT F. GIAMMONA ‖ DEBRA L. GIBBON ✠FF. JAMES A. GIBERSON ‖ CRAIG NEIL GIBSON ✠LT. RONNIE E. GIES ‖ LAURA A. GION ✠LT
CK ‖ JOHN T. GNAZZO ‖ WILLIAM 'BILL' ROBERT GODSHALK ‖ MICHAEL GOGLIORMELLA ‖ BRIAN FREDRIC GOLDBERG ‖ JEFFREY GRANT GOLDFLAM ‖ MIERG ‖ RRG ‖
GRADY ‖ EDWIN JOHN GRAF III ‖ DAVID M. GRAIFMAN ‖ GILBERT GRANADOS ‖ ELVIRA GRANITTO ‖ WINSTON ARTHUR GRANT ‖ CHRISTOPHER STEWART GUR GRRR GR
EF JOSEPH GRZELAK ‖ MATTHEW J. GRZYMALSKI ‖ ROBERT JOSEPH GSCHAAR ‖ LIMING 'MICHAEL' GU ✠FF. JOSE A. GUADALUPE ‖ YAN ZHU 'CINDY' GE A. G A. G
ELICIA HAMILTON ✠FF. ROBERT W. HAMILTON ‖ FREDERIC KIM HAN ‖ MOHAMMED HANDANI EMS ‖ CHRISTOPHER JAMES HANLEY ✠FF. SEAN S. HAHER JHER
NARD WILLIAM HATTON ✠FF. MICHAEL HELMUT HAUB ‖ TIMOTHY AARON HAVILAND ‖ DONALD G. HAVLISH ‖ ANTHONY HAWKINS ‖ NOBUHIRO HAYATSNTHONTHON
L HERNANDEZ ‖ NORBERTO HERNANDEZ ‖ RAUL HERNANDEZ ‖ GARY HEROLD ‖ JEFFREY A. HERSCH ✠FF. THOMAS J. HETZEL ✠BAT. CHIEF BRIAN HIGMAS JJAS J
OHMANN ‖ JOSEPH FRANCIS HOLLAND ‖ JOHN HOLLAND ‖ ELIZABETH HOLMES ✠FF. THOMAS P. HOLOHAN ‖ BRADLEY HOORN ‖ JAMES P. HOPPER ‖ MONLEY HEEY H
R ‖ ROBERT HUSSA ✠CAPT. WALTER G. HYNES ‖ THOMAS E. HYNES ‖ JOSEPH ANTHONY IANELLI ‖ ZUHTU IBIS ✠FF. JONATHAN LEE IELPI ‖ MICHAEL PATR. JON. J JON
SON ‖ RICKNAUTH JAGGERNAUTH ‖ JAKE DENIS JAGODA ‖ YUDH V.S. JAIN ‖ MARIA JAKUBIAK ‖ GRICELDA E. JAMES ‖ ERNEST JAMES ‖ MARK S. JAJAMESAME
AS JORDAN ‖ STEPHEN JOSEPH ‖ INGEBORG JOSEPH ✠FF. KARL HENRI JOSEPH ‖ ALBERT JOSEPH ‖ JANE EILEEN JOSIAH ✠LT. ANTHONY M. JOVIC LEEN JEEN J
NDREW KATES ‖ JOHN KATSIMATIDES ✠SGT. ROBERT KAULFERS ‖ DON JEROME KAUTH ‖ HIDEYA KAWAUCHI ‖ EDWARD T. KEANE ‖ RICHARD M. KEANEDWARDWA
KETCHAM ‖ RUTH E. KETLER ‖ BORIS KHALIF ‖ SARAH KHAN ‖ TAIMOUR FIRAZ KHAN ‖ RAJESH KHANDELWAL ‖ SEILAI KHOO ✠FF. MICHAEL V. KIEFE SEIL S SEI
ESTNER ‖ RYAN KOHART ‖ VANESSA LYNN KOLPAK ‖ IRINA KOLPAKOVA ‖ SUZANNE KONDRATENKO ‖ ABDOULAYE KONE ‖ BON-SEOK KOO ‖ DOROTA KOE KONEKKON
AFRANCE ‖ JUAN LAFUENTE ‖ NEIL K. LAI ‖ VINCENT A. LAIETA ✠FF. WILLIAM DAVID LAKE ‖ FRANCO LALAMA ‖ CHOW KWAN LAM ‖ STEPHEN LAMA ‖ CHO C CH
N ‖ STEPHEN JAMES LAURIA ‖ MARIA LAVACHE ‖ DENIS F. LAVELLE ‖ JEANNINE M. LAVERDE ‖ ANNA A. LAVERTY ‖ STEVEN LAWN ‖ ROBERT A. LAWRITY ‖ SY / ‖ S
✠PO. DAVID PRUDENCIO LEMAGNE ‖ JOSEPH A. LENIHAN ✠PO. JOHN J. LENNON ‖ JOHN ROBINSON LENOIR ‖ JORGE LUIS LEON ‖ MATTHEW GERARJORGEDRGE
NE ‖ ALAN LINTON ‖ DIANE THERESA LIPARI ‖ KENNETH P. LIRA ‖ FRANCISCO ALBERTO LIRIANO ‖ LORRAINE LISI ‖ PAUL LISSON ‖ VINCENT LITTO ‖ MISI ‖ PSISI
THOMAS LUGANO ‖ DANIEL LUGO ‖ MARIE LUKAS ‖ WILLIAM LUM ‖ MICHAEL P. LUNDEN ‖ CHRISTOPHER LUNDER ‖ ANTHONY LUPARELLO ‖ GARY LUER ‖ ARR ‖ A
RLES WILSON MAGEE ‖ BRIAN MAGEE ‖ JOSEPH V. MAGGITTI ‖ RONALD E. MAGNUSON ‖ DANIEL L. MAHER ‖ THOMAS ANTHONY MAHON ✠FF. WILLIAMOMAS MMAS
VICH ✠LT. CHARLES JOSEPH MARGIOTTA ✠FF. KENNETH JOSEPH MARINO ‖ LESTER VINCENT MARINO ‖ VITA MARINO ‖ KEVIN D. MARLO ‖ JOSE J. MARRINO RRINO
VILLIAM A. MATHESEN ‖ MARCELLO MATRICCIANO ‖ MARGARET ELAINE MATTIC ‖ ROBERT D. MATTSON ‖ WALTER MATUZA ‖ CHARLES A. 'CHUCK' MER MARR M
‖ STANLEY MCCASKILL ‖ KATIE MARIE MCCLOSKEY ‖ TARA MCCLOUD-GRAY ‖ CHARLES AUSTIN MCCRANN ‖ TONYELL MCDAY ‖ MATTHEW T. MCDEONYEDNNYE
UGH ‖ ANN M. MCHUGH ‖ ROBERT G. MCILVAINE ✠PO. DONALD JAMES MCINTYRE ‖ STEPHANIE MCKENNA ‖ BARRY J. MCKEON ‖ EVELYN C. MCKINNERRY J.RRY J
R MEHTA ✠FF. RAYMOND M. MEISENHEIMER ‖ MANUEL EMILIO MEJIA ‖ ESKEDAR MELAKU ‖ ANTONIO MELENDEZ ‖ MARY MELENDEZ ‖ YELENA MELNICH ‖ MAR I MA
MILLER, JR. ‖ PHILLIP D. MILLER ‖ CRAIG JAMES MILLER ‖ COREY PETER MILLER ✠FF. DOUGLAS C. MILLER ‖ MICHAEL MATTHEW MILLER ‖ ROBERT C. CHAELHHAEL
KLEBER ROLANDO MOLINA ✠FF. CARL E. MOLINARO ‖ JUSTIN J. MOLISANI ‖ BRIAN PATRICK MONAGHAN ‖ FRANKLIN MONAHAN ‖ JOHN GERARD MONAKLIN MLILIN
MOROCHO ‖ LEONEL MOROCHO ‖ DENNIS G. MORONEY ‖ LYNNE IRENE MORRIS ‖ SETH A. MORRIS ‖ STEPHEN PHILIP MORRIS ‖ CHRISTOPHER M. MORRHILIP M LIP
URILLO ‖ MARC A. MUROLO ‖ ROBERT EDDIE MURPHY ‖ BRIAN JOSEPH MURPHY ‖ CHRISTOPHER W. MURPHY ‖ EDWARD C. MURPHY ‖ JAMES F. MURPHEDWARDWA
. NEBLETT ‖ JEROME O. NEDD ‖ LAURENCE NEDELL ‖ LUKE G. NEE ‖ PETE NEGRON ‖ ANN NICOLE NELSON ‖ DAVID WILLIAM NELSON ✠PO. JAMES NAVID W.VID
A ‖ JOSE R. NUNEZ ‖ BRIAN FELIX NUNEZ ‖ JEFFREY NUSSBAUM ‖ JAMES A. OAKLEY ✠FF. DENNIS P. O'BERG ‖ TIMOTHY MICHAEL O'BRIEN ‖ JAMES P. TIMOTIMMO
OLINA OSORIO OLIVA ‖ LINDA MARY OLIVA ‖ EDWARD K. OLIVER ‖ LEAH E. OLIVER ✠FF. ERIC T. OLSEN ✠FF. JEFFREY JAMES OLSEN ‖ MAUREEN L. OLSFREY JRREY
OTHY O'SULLIVAN ‖ JASON DOUGLAS OSWALD ✠FF. MICHAEL J. OTTEN ‖ ISIDRO OTTENWALDER ‖ MICHAEL CHUNG OU ‖ TODD JOSEPH OUIDA ‖ JESUS ONG OU G OU
MSOTHY ‖ NITIN RAMESH PARANDKAR ‖ HARDAI 'CASEY' PARBHU ✠PO. JAMES WENDELL PARHAM ‖ DEBRA 'DEBBIE' PARIS ‖ GEORGE PARIS ‖ GYE-HYOBBIE' FBBIE'
AUL ‖ SHARON CRISTINA MILLAN PAZ ‖ PATRICE PAZ ‖ VICTOR PAZ-GUTIERREZ ‖ STACEY L. PEAK ✚EMT RICHARD ALLEN PEARLMAN ✠FF. DURRELL V. PEALLENLLLE
RUSSEL PETERSON ‖ MARK PETROCELLI ✠LT. PHILIP S. PETTI ✠PO. GLEN KERRIN PETTIT ✠PO. DOMINICK A. PEZZULO ‖ KALEEN E. PEZZUTI ✠LT. KEVIZULOZZULO
S ‖ STEVE POLLICINO ‖ SUSAN M. POLLIO ‖ JOSHUA POPTEAN ‖ GIOVANNA PORRAS ‖ ANTHONY PORTILLO ‖ JAMES EDWARD POTORTI ‖ DAPHNE POUMES EEES E
NN QUIGLEY ✠LT. MICHAEL T. QUILTY ✚EMT RICARDO QUINN EMS ‖ JAMES FRANCIS QUINN ‖ CAROL RABALAIS ‖ CHRISTOPHER PETER A. RACANIELL ‖ CHI ‖ CH
ARK RASWEILER ‖ DAVID ALAN JAMES RATHKEY ‖ WILLIAM RALPH RAUB ‖ GERARD RAUZI ‖ ALEXEY RAZUVAEV ‖ GREGORY REDA ‖ SARAH PROTHERO ‖ GRE ‖ GR
RICCARDELLI ‖ RUDOLPH N. RICCIO ‖ ANNMARIE 'DAVI' RICCOBONI ‖ EILEEN MARY RICE ‖ DAVID RICE ‖ KENNETH F. RICE ✠CAPT. VERNON ALLAN RETH F.TTH F
SON ‖ JEFFREY ROBINSON ‖ CATHERINA ROBINSON ‖ MICHELL LEE ROBOTHAM ‖ DONALD ROBSON ‖ ANTONIO AUGUSTO TOME ROCHA ‖ RAYMOND J. RAUGUSTOGUS
‖ MARK H. ROSEN ‖ LINDA ROSENBAUM ‖ BROOKE DAVID ROSENBAUM ‖ SHERYL LYNN ROSENBAUM ‖ LLOYD D. ROSENBERG ‖ MARK LOUIS ROSENBERROSERROSE
O ‖ JOHN J. RYAN ‖ EDWARD RYAN ‖ JONATHAN STEPHAN RYAN ✠BAT. CHIEF MATTHEW LANCELOT RYAN ‖ KRISTIN A. IRVINE RYAN ‖ TATIANA RYJOVISTIN ATIN
M-DINNOO ‖ JAMES KENNETH SAMUEL ‖ HUGO SANAY-PERAFIEL ‖ ERICK SANCHEZ ‖ ALVA JEFFRIES SANCHEZ ‖ JACQUELYN P. SANCHEZ ‖ ERIC SAND ‖ JACQ JAC
FF. JOHN A. SCHARDT ‖ JOHN G. SCHARF ✠BAT. CHIEF FRED CLAUDE SCHEFFOLD ‖ ANGELA SUSAN SCHEINBERG ‖ SCOTT M. SCHERTZER ‖ SEAN SCHIE ‖ SCO ‖ SC
CARLOS SEGARRA ‖ ANTHONY SEGARRA ‖ JASON SEKZER ‖ MATTHEW CARMEN SELLITTO ‖ HOWARD SELWYN ‖ LARRY JOHN SENKO ‖ ARTURO ANGELO SERRY JERRY J
MARK SHULMAN ‖ SEE-WONG SHUM ‖ ALLAN SHWARTZSTEIN ‖ JOHANNA SIGMUND ‖ DIANNE T. SIGNER ✠FF. GREGORY R. SIKORSKY ✠FF. STEPHEN GREGOREGO
N ‖ ROBERT SLIWAK ‖ PAUL K. SLOAN ✠FF. STANLEY S. SMAGALA, JR. ‖ WENDY L. SMALL ‖ CATHERINE T. SMITH ‖ DANIEL LAURENCE SMITH ‖ GEORGE E ‖ DANIDDAN
ARO ✠FF. ROBERT W. SPEAR, JR. ‖ MAYNARD S. SPENCE ‖ GEORGE E. SPENCER ‖ ROBERT ANDREW SPENCER ‖ MARY RUBINA SPERANDO ‖ FRANK ‖ MAI ‖ MA
NDER ROBBINS STEINMAN ‖ ANDREW STERGIOPOULOS ‖ ANDREW STERN ‖ MARTHA JANE STEVENS ‖ RICHARD H. STEWART ‖ MICHAEL JAMES STEVD H. SH. S
EPH SUOZZO ‖ COLLEEN SUPINSKI ‖ ROBERT SUTCLIFFE ‖ SELINA SUTTER ‖ CLAUDIA SUZETTE SUTTON ‖ JOHN F. SWAINE ‖ KRISTINE M. SWEARSON F. SWA S SWA
JR. ‖ KENNETH JOSEPH TARANTINO ✠FF. ALLAN TARASIEWICZ ‖ RONALD TARTARO ‖ DARRYL TAYLOR ‖ DONNIE BROOKS TAYLOR, SR. ‖ LORISA CEYLON BROOKROO
. JOHN PATRICK TIERNEY ‖ MARY ELLEN TIESI ‖ WILLIAM R. TIESTE ✠PO. KENNETH F. TIETJEN ‖ STEPHEN EDWARD TIGHE ‖ SCOTT C. TIMMES ‖ MICHAERD TIGD TI
SEPH TROMBINO ‖ GREGORY J. TROST ‖ WILLIAM TSELEPIS ‖ ZHANETTA TSOY ‖ MICHAEL PATRICK TUCKER ‖ LANCE RICHARD TUMULTY ‖ CHING PING TNCE RICEE R
RICK T. VARACCHI ‖ GOPALAKRISHNAN VARADHAN ‖ DAVID VARGAS ‖ SCOTT C. VASEL ‖ SANTOS VASQUEZ ‖ AZAEL ISMAEL VASQUEZ ‖ ARCANGEL VAZQUL ISMAISMA
VOLA ‖ LYNETTE D. VOSGES ‖ GARO H. VOSKERIJIAN ‖ ALFRED VUKOSA ‖ GREGORY WACHTLER ‖ GABRIELA WAISMAN ‖ WENDY ALICE ROSARIO WAKEFOMAN ‖ AAN ‖
ATRICK J. WATERS II ✠FF. KENNETH T. WATSON ‖ MICHAEL H. WAYE ✠PO. WALTER E. WEAVER ‖ TODD C. WEAVER ✠PO. NATHANIEL WEBB ‖ DINAH WER ✠PRR ✠
SA WHITE ‖ WAYNE WHITE ‖ ADAM S. WHITE ‖ LEANNE MARIE WHITESIDE ✠FF. MARK P. WHITFORD ✠PO. MICHAEL T. WHOLEY ‖ MARY LENZ WIEMANAEL TABEL
TTENSTEIN ‖ CHRISTOPHER W. WODENSHEK ‖ MARTIN PHILLIPS 'BUFF' WOHLFORTH ‖ KATHERINE S. WOLF ‖ JENNY SEU KUENG LOW WONG ‖ YUK PINNNY SINNY
‖ SUZANNE YOUMANS ‖ JACQUELINE 'JAKKI' YOUNG ‖ BARRINGTON L. YOUNG ‖ ELKIN YUEN ‖ JOSEPH ZACCOLI ‖ ADEL AGAYBY ZAKHARY ‖ ARKADY ZALTADEL ADEL
LEWIS ✈ RENEE A. MAY ✈ PAUL AMBROSE ✈ YENENEH BETRU ✈ MARY JANE 'MJ' BOOTH ✈ BERNARD CURTIS BROWN ✈ SUZANNE CALLEY ✈ WILLIAMBROWNCOWN
BARBARA OLSON ✈ RUBEN ORNEDO ✈ ROBERT PENNIGER ✈ ROBERT R. PLOGER ✈ LISA J. RAINES ✈ TODD REUBEN ✈ JOHN SAMMARTINO ✈ MARTINENERJUBE
LANDO CALDERON-OLMEDO ✪ ANGELENE C. CARTER ✪ SHARON CARVER ✪ JOHN J. CHADA ✪ ROSA MARIA 'ROSEMARY' CHAPA ✪ JULIAN COOPER ✪ COMARY' AARY
EILA HEIN ✪ RONALD JOHN HEMENWAY ✪ MAJ. WALLACE COLE HOGAN ✪ JIMMIE IRA HOLLEY ✪ ANGELA HOUTZ ✪ BRADY K. HOWELL ✪ PEGGIE HURTEGGIEBRADYRRAD
V. MORRIS ✪ BRIAN ANTHONY MOSS ✪ TED MOY ✪ LT. CMDR. PATRICK JUDE MURPHY ✪ KHANG NGUYEN ✪ MICHAEL ALLEN NOETH ✪ DIANA BORRERNA BOL ALLEALLE
N SERVA ✪ CMDR. DAN FREDERIC SHANOWER ✪ ANTOINETTE SHERMAN ✪ DON SIMMONS ✪ CHERYLE D. SINCOCK ✪ GREGG HAROLD SMALLWOOD MALLY ✪ GRI ✪ GRI
✈ FLIGHT 93 ✈ LORRAINE G. BAY ✈ SANDRA W. BRADSHAW ✈ JASON DAHL ✈ WANDA ANITA GREEN ✈ LEROY HOMER ✈ CEECEE LYLES ✈ DEBYLES ✈ HOMEHOME
EAN HOADLEY PETERSON ✈ WALESKA MARTINEZ RIVERA ✈ MARK ROTHENBERG ✈ CHRISTINE SNYDER ✈ JOHN TALIGNANI ✈ HONOR ELIZABETH WAINABETHGNANINNAN

The Millenium Hilton

On September 11, 2001, I was on my way back to work when I saw the first airplane fly into the building; that tragedy sent me into a depression and stress.

So, I decided to volunteer and these days I spend my time distributing history books so that we will never forget. Visitors from all over the globe come to see the site and are reminded of the loss but also get to see the new building and the hope of a new tomorrow.

23

24

The Sphere

A sculpture that survived the 9/11 attacks on the World Trade Center was recovered from the rubble. It now resides in Battery Park.

Father Brian Jordan, second from left, blesses, Thursday, Oct. 4, 2001, a cross of steel beams found amidst the rubble of the World Trade Center by a laborer two days after the collapse of the twin towers. The cross was from World Trade tower One, and was found in World Trade building Six and moved to its present location Wednesday. Other rescue and construction workers join Jordan for the ceremony. A protective mesh hangs on the building in the background. (AP Photo/Pool, Kathy Willens)

Within hours of the Sept. 11 attacks, thousands of rescue workers from across America deployed to ground zero to help in the search and rescue efforts. Joining the endeavor, were dogs specially trained in search and rescue, police work, therapy and comfort. It is estimated that more than 300 dogs took part in the search, rescue and recovery efforts at Ground Zero.

Search and rescue dogs (SAR) specialize in disaster response skills. Trained to search and detect the scent of living humans, their mission was to find survivors buried in the rubble. The last living person rescued from Ground Zero 27 hours after the collapse was found by one of these search and rescue dogs.

Vesey St.

View down W Broadway toward Vesey St. WTC 7 on right. Fires observed from WTC 7. WTC 5 is visible across Vesey S with WTC 6 visible. Vesey Street bridge can also be seen.

Winter Garden Atrium

The Atrium was severely damaged in the September 11, 2001 attacks as almost all the glass panes were blown out by the dust clouds and debris caused by the collapse of the Twin Towers.

"One of the worst days in America's history saw some of the bravest acts in Americans' history. We'll always honor the heroes of 9/11. And here at this hallowed place, we pledge that we will never forget their sacrifice."
- Former President George W. Bush.

ONE WORL
TRADE CENTE
FREEDOM TOWE

1,776 FT. TALL (541 M.)
1 WTC – 104 STORIES

2 WTC – 80+ STORIES

3 WTC – 80 STORIES

4 WTC – 72 STORIES

7 WTC –
52 STORIES

32